# The Great American Poetry Show

# The Great American Poetry Show

Volume 2

edited
by

**Larry Ziman**
**Madeline Sharples**
**Nicky Selditz**

**The Muse Media**
**West Hollywood**

# The Great American Poetry Show

Published by:
The Muse Media
Post Office Box 69506
West Hollywood, California 90069

Contributing Editor: Steve Goldman

Volume 2: Copyright © 2010 by Larry Ziman
Cover Design: Copyright © 2010 by Larry Ziman

Library of Congress Control Number: 2009912400
ISBN 978-0-933456-06-8
ISSN 1550-0527

Printed by:
Thomson-Shore, Inc.
7300 West Joy Road
Dexter, Michigan 48130-9701

Text set in Plantin and printed on acid-free paper
First Edition - First Printing: 1000 copies, July 2010

Manufactured in the United States of America

*The Great American Poetry Show* is a serial poetry anthology open year-round to submissions of poems in English on any subject and in any style, length and number either by email or by mail with a self-addressed stamped envelope. Mailed submissions without a self-addressed stamped envelope will be discarded. Simultaneous submissions and previously published poems are welcome.

The Great American Poetry Show
Post Office Box 69506
West Hollywood, California 90069

Email: info@tgaps.net
Website: www.tgaps.net
Telephone: 323-656-6126

# The Great American Poetry Show

# The Great American Poetry Show

# The Great American Poetry Show

## A Short History Of Imperialism

Her desire to be a tyrant
matched his need
to be an occupied nation.

Still, the history of revolution
teaches that even the most docile populations
have an eventual tipping point.

"You forgot to empty the dishwasher,"
she said, her tone impatient,
annoyed, dismissive.

He grabbed the remote and raised
the volume, drowning her out.
The insurrection had begun.

**Chuck Augello**

## Que Dios le Bendiga

We meet on an empty road, in the dry season
of my life,
    the *abuela* and I.

She reaches for me with *manos viejos*,
gnarled by work, twisted by polio—double curses,
neither escapable—yet hands still strong
    with the grip of life.

And when these hands grab mine (hers
the givers of breast, bean, and tortilla
to the mouths of *niños*),
    she speaks:

*Que Dios le bendiga,*

that God would bless thee, a prosaic greeting
following the impress of flesh, the proper
way for the old to yield their blessing
    to the young, to a stranger.

But though she releases my hands,
I cannot let go of hers.  As if holding
a live wire, I grip tighter, clinging

to her on this forlorn road
while fleeting universes
yawn—mystery's curtain
for a moment rent—in this sheltering
place, in this holding of hands.

**Fred Bahnson**

## This Is How

At dawn I hold the lamb for him.  First lulled
by warmth, I recoil when his knife opens
its throat, when its legs flail, slow, then pulse

against mine.  The blood—
sticky on my hands.  Bleats turn to moans
turn to silence.  This is how

we kill in Zimbabwe.  He shows me how
to retract the head, baring
the throat.  This is how the Hebrews kill;

first the artery, then the spinal cord.
He tells how the killing was done
to his own, how one day soldiers razed his village,

forced him to watch them bind his sister, his only sister—
lovely as a gazelle, pure as a lamb—
before coming for him.  This is how

you make the cut.  He spreads his fingers
into a V, easing the knife between, separating
skin from abdomen, foreleg from shoulder, careful

that not one bone be broken.  His voice—
serene yet resistant.  On him
they cut tendons, then other parts.  We are into this now,

slicing and pulling, forearm deep in gore, washing out
intestines before the heat comes.  I take the blade
in haste, cut deep into the wrong flesh,

my own blood joining
the other.  I press hard until
the bleeding stops, and we work on.

Late morning when the knives
are cleaned, when the lamb has been
prepared for the feast, he asks

for my hand, works in stinging
ointment, says: This is how
we help the wound to mend.

**Fred Bahnson**

3

## Yankee Lake

*Couldn't see your hand*
*before your face.*
First time I heard it was
that summer at Yankee Lake.

Jay said it.  Each dawn
as we slept in the damp
cabin, he put on fishing clothes
& left, pulling the oars
of the painted boat, vanishing

into the mountain fog, metallic
& thick as dust, yet exhilarating,
I think, for him.  If he caught
a fish we ate it.  If he didn't,
we didn't.  Catching the fish wasn't

the point.  The point was taking
his seventeen-year-old self
out on the lake, to sit in the
quiet morning, hear the water
kiss the gunwales,

see the murk turn from sienna to
yellow to gold, feel the sun, finally,
on his cheek, below his twill hat,
& think his thoughts, humming
to himself.  He did not will or wish

the fish to bite.  If they did, fine,
If they didn't, okay.  He'd had his
solitude, made his own way
to start the day.  I don't know.
All I know is he took himself

away from us, to float on the
water, to experience a kind of
heaven he rowed himself to.  The
first of many departures from us,
until he left, abruptly, in an

April full of gold & tulips,
so that I still think
he isn't vanished, just out on
the lake, in the early morning,
fishing.

**Gay Baines**

## Vanishing Point

The wind is a steady hand at my chest.
An hour to ride my bike head-first
into spring, that flimsy catkin teasing
from a maple, the thing I follow
at a lumbering, hypnotic cadence.
I push through early-morning shadows
and winter's left-over gloom
as the sun winnows down the path.

Nothing distracts but the juncos
criss-crossing like lace unraveling.
Behind me, three miles by now,
my child busies the dust
in the hulking house, the place
where all of this began.
I long to be no longer visible, an arrow
quivering into a grove but missing
every tree, an exquisite passing.

Below a frost-slicked trestle,
the creek swells its green skin
with yesterday's pollen and rain.
A fresh grave is being dug on the hill.
Skunk cabbage jaws open above
the curved rot of a lone Chinook
in the shallows.  Cottonwood resin
coats the air, sweet and welcome.

From the mottled water, a mallard
pads her way up the mud bank
to a nest enfolded
by ten hues of green.  So clearly
she slips into the tangle
while her mate devotedly treads
in the direction of her return.

Like the expected rioting
of bud to flower to fruit,
I am unable to resist the path.
The wind, now at my back,
chills my bare legs revolving out
a rhythm that will carry me homeward.
Iron-hot blood floods
its capillarious routes.  Propelled,
I become that point
on the horizon slowly
coming back into view.

**Kristin Berger**

## The Professor

Once he was an academic man;
Now he studies green flock wallpaper.
During daylight hours he sits transfixed
In his damp-resistant plastic chair.
Perhaps it is the fleur-de-lys, embossed;
French history was his speciality.

Once he wore a gown and mortarboard;
Now he'd go naked if they let him.
It's not 'Professor' any more
But 'pet' and 'dear' and first-name terms
From kids who come on work experience
And supervise him in the lavatory.

Once he enthralled crowded lecture halls;
Now he waits, incontinence padded,
Receiving dosages of Coronation Street.
He was seen to smile last Wednesday.
They thought it was something Dierdre said
But Matron reckoned it was flatulence.

Once he bestrode a famous campus;
Now he needs a care assistant's help
To find his room along the corridor.
They used to let him go alone
Until Miss Philpott found him in her bed.
Fortunately she knew him long before.

Once he dreamed his name would be revered;
Now he can't remember what it is.
Most often he is Bonaparte or Metternich,
Ignoble footnotes to a history man.
But nice Mrs Blenkinsop seems to understand;
For quite a while she's been the Virgin Mary.

Once he published learned papers;
Now he puzzles over signs on toilet doors.
Yet in the green room afternoons
He silently gathers in the tricks,
And his regular partners rejoice.
Somewhere a candle flickers still.

John C Bird

## At Either End of the Web

*"Man did not weave the web of life, he is merely a strand in it.
Whatever he does to the web, he does to himself."* Chief Sealth

She spins by moonlight,
weaving wet strands
from mailbox to brass knob,
binding my door shut with her silk.

Each morning I claw at the web,
unraveling her mending from the night
before.  She watches from behind
a clapboard, waits for darkness.

What is this web to her
that she will not surrender
but will patiently repair my damage?
Am I connected to its strands

like the crumpled moth trapped
in the sticky tangle in my hand
or like a nightmare snared
in a dream-catcher? What is this thing

I rip apart – some kind of primitive
survival map whose language has been lost
to me? Just as her instinct is to claim
this space, mine is to tear down obstacles.

Neither of us will back down.  One has to go,
be banished from this struggle over territory.
Perhaps this is the way all wars begin –
small battles fought in strands of gossamer.

**Regina Murray Brault**

## Process of Elimination

As he arranges his closet,
the number of items left
dwindles with each pass.
The navy wool sweater that
SHE gave him for Valentine's
should go, along with the
tan leather travel kit SHE picked out
for the trip they never took,
and the photo of them, embracing,
after a Stones concert last winter.

Yes, these can go, he thinks,
as can the paisley socks he bought
because it's HER favorite pattern.
Oh, and the Cole Haan boots
he wore on their fifth date,
until they were removed
along with belt, pants, and shirt,
in favor of a natural state where
two bodies enmeshed, rolling
and heaving and sweating until
crisp white cotton sheets reduced
to a damp, irreverent ball.
All of this reminding him that
the bedding, too, must go.

When everything is decided upon,
culled down, thrown away,
all he's left with is the skin that
once pressed against hers,
the lips that consumed her own,
and other parts her body
had so eagerly enveloped.
What will he do with these?

**Susan Breeden**

## Amtrak Overnight

Whoever pinned stars against the L.A. night
holds me captive in a window seat
until the desert mountains show their teeth.

Joshuas raise arms
like followers of Vodoun,
performing sacred rites along the tracks.

Hunted creatures creep beneath the sage,
lying low, drawing unnoticed conclusions
about surviving time and space.

Hesitant serpents complain,
tongues traversing the four directions,
stalking last light
through trailer parks.

An occasional cloud of dust
appears at my window
to roll unsettled eyes,
then vanish.

A late watch of nightingale
sings to us at a rest stop, restoring
order in the grip of electric wires.

Sleep, an obsessed thief
whose time is running out,
interferes with my meditations.

Consciousness gets lost
attempting astral flight
at the faltering speed of a train.

An angry woman, having
somehow soaked her only pair of socks
in cream soda,
rages into my sleep.

Unfamiliar men, painfully
young and drunk on absurdity,
play dominoes 'til dawn.

Restless children
begin to dance with
daylight and coloring books
on the leading edge of New Mexico.

Outside my window, mesquite
and mourning dove
listen to a steel train cry at sunrise.

The scalding surface
of a cup of coffee, at my touch,
trembles through a long curve.

**Don Brennan**

## Oolong

In the land of honey and four kinds of milk
        a man on the sidewalk
        stares through the window
        of the House of Oolong.
Between sips of tea
        I stare back at lips discernibly mobile,
        a face roughly shaven,
        eyebrows in a knot.
Is he rehearsing a panhandle line, composing
        a prayer to an overwrought god, just as likely
        talking to himself?
On this side of the Oolong window
        half and half puddles
        at the foot of a black pot,
        honey waits to be squeezed
        from plastic bears.
I am able to discern the motion
        but not the noise of a stranger's lips;
Not knowing from his vague eyes
        if he is even speaking to me,
        creating words by the thump of a heart
pumping blood-borne precursors of speech
        through a capillary net deep beneath
        his shaggy hair and stocking cap
to flow there into consonants and vowels
        and gather like the drip of honey and
        milk at the tip of a tongue.
His mental molecules become words in ways
        I can't imagine,
but whatever he might have to say,
        perhaps brilliant or absurd or both,
        remains unheard.
The man's speech stalls in arrested flight
        against the outside glass
        of the House of Oolong.
I notice on my table a fly's futile struggle
        to escape the sticky grip of a honey bear
        as I sip my tea and ponder mysteries
        of the spoken word.

**Don Brennan**

**The Old Toad**

This old toad
spotted me
couple nights ago
returning
from recycling bottles and aluminum cans
at the curb.

He thought he could
imitate a rock,
but I knew
it was him,
shoulders
wrinkled
above his muscular, gold-speckled back.

Distracted, I
swiveled my head
briefly
toward a
snap of twigs
in thick, October darkness.

But when I swiveled
back,
I noticed immediately
that my dear old friend
had quietly
relocated himself
entirely
inside
a pitch-black shadow
just below
the patio lattice.

**Alan Britt**

## Travels with Jack

Jack Benny is passing
from the solar system
to the outer stars,
The Shadow right behind him,
carried on radio waves
that, once released to space,
continue to drift forever.

The girl is with them,
her hands on her chin,
her stomach on the floor.
She listens alone,
pictures hovering in her head.

She is with them now
as they were with her
in Wyoming, in Alberta, in Calgary,
wherever a distracted father,
intent on building an empire
of machine shops, temporarily
planted her.

She laughs at Bob Hope.
She is surprised to hear
that Amos 'n Andy are white.
She listens to the President
talk about the Good War.

She travels with them past Pluto,
heading for parts unknown
as her family has done so often.
She listens as her parents fight,
as her father hits her mother again
always, always when
the girl is there to see it.

No, she's not there.
She travels at the speed of sound
with Jack and The Shadow
who knows what evil
lurks in the hearts of men.
She, too, knows
but keeps it secret

like her own identity
and the way she turns aside
a personal question with a joke
to cloud men's minds.

She lives in the same house
with the same husband now
for thirty years.  But she's still
a girl, stomach on the floor,
vibrations of the radio
humming through her bones,

lifting her, lifting her
past Saturn and Jupiter,
out past Pluto where Jack Benny
has just asked Rochester
to bring the car around
for another long trip
into eternity.

**MCBruce**

**Doing Interstate 27**

With the lights out,
she's hypnotic.
You have to catch yourself every once in a while,
as each curve can kill a man
and every sign is an innuendo.

But you soon see that she
is a relentless dry-hump
with no rest at all
and no climax.

She leaves you sore and angry.

Interstate 27 is a bump and grind.
It's a long stretch to nowhere
and a futile quest for a place to let.

She is an asphalt whore
with nothing to consider but death and dying.

At daybreak
you feel used and sick to your stomach.
You're just another pop
for this moaning bitch
who's as stupid as she is ugly.

And yet, hanging over her head (when the lights are out)
are constellations so beautiful they take your breath away.

She may be hard on the eyes,
but she sure knows how to decorate.

I'll give her that.

**Howard Camner**

**My Mentor**

My mentor sits
staring at a painting on his wall.
It is a painting of a giant face.
A giant face with no eyes, no mouth, no nose, no ears,
nothing.
It's just a blank face.
My mentor just stares at it
all day and all night.
I visit him once a week for inspiration.
He never looks at me.
He just stares at the painting of the blank face
and imparts his wisdom:
"The nail that holds this painting up on the wall
never gets a moment's rest.  Don't be a nail."

**Howard Camner**

**To My Daughter on a Fine Fall Day**

I stand behind you and push,
harder and harder.
You pump higher.
Feet kick the air.
You swing back,
just miss my arms
waiting to receive you.
Hands fall to my sides,
hide themselves in coat pockets.

You're over the sandbox
filled now with maple leaves.
Shoes skim the hedge,
reach past this boundary line.
You lie in your bed of air,
no pillows for your head.

I watch you wake,
hanging there above me,
a sparrow in its nest.
Your fingers clutch the chains,
probe the links,
let go the hold.
You jump, splitting the noonday sun.
I cannot stop your feet from touching ground.

**Carol Carpenter**

### Wicker Chair & Coreopsis

My mother left this white wicker chair
to me who knew the intricacy of the weave,
the way each strand overlapped
and wrapped over and under itself,
creating the pattern of us.

There in her private place I listened
when she hummed like the wind rustling leaves
in the plum tree.  She whistled sparrows to the ground:
t-weet, t-weet, t-weet.  She could make me hear
the rise and fall of butterfly wings in air.

Mother kept her sewing basket full of thread
on the white wicker table.  All colors
moved through the eye of her needle:  the deep blue
of a jay's wing feather, the red of her blazing roses
climbing the fence, the white of clouds shifting shape.

From pieces of fabric, she designed my clothes,
knowing what would fit, what would bring out
my coloring, what would move with me like skin
when I was ten and growing faster than grass.
She sewed me into myself, leaving seams to let out.

I watched her fingers move, the needle flash in
and out of cloth as she turned flat flowered cotton
into a full skirt buttoned at the waist.  She was
a magician who taught me how to sit quietly and wait
for coreopsis buds to open into gold suns at our feet.

Every year the coreopsis bloom on the same day
and I place the white wicker chair and table just right.
Light weaves my mother's shape in that quiet space
and I hum along with mother's songs, hear leaves fall
as mother performs her magic tricks and all is an illusion.

**Carol Carpenter**

## Iron

After twenty-four days in County
he was close to raving, climbing
the walls whacked, unable to sit
still, totally getting on everyone's
nerves. Telling him to slow down
only made him more hyper, got him
marked for a beating or a shiv, maybe
both at the same time, something
the guards thought he was earning,
always acting out in overdrive,
spacey as an astronaut on nitrous.
"That dude is totally out of control,"
his cellmate would complain.
No one could actually recall
seeing him at rest as in reasonably
inert or asleep, occasionally stationary,
maybe, when he was visiting the head.
It was understood that a man like him
couldn't read. Television bored the hell
out of him. Movies were for droolers
though he did express an interest in
hardcore pornography, the kind whose
subject matter usually earned you more
than six months in County even knowing
of its existence. Some speculated that
he must have something heavy pending
on the outside that cooling his heels
behind bars was keeping on hold,
the kind of delay that could get a man
killed or worse. Once when he said,
"This is just like the army, FUBAR city,"
 he freaked his cellie totally out.
"Aint no FUBAR in here," cellie said.
"That's what you think."
"Well, FUBAR this," cellie said,
swinging an iron weight in a bath towel
directly into his face.

Alan Catlin

## No-Tell-Motel Ship of Fools

They show in-house Girls-Gone-Wild
pornos easily accessed for a nominal
fee, no questions asked, no ID's checked,
and they wonder why naked guys jump
from fifth-floor windows in the general
direction of the pool, clutching empty
cheap champagne bottles in either hand,
and end up dead, a messy floater no one
wants to wake up to. They pretend
amazement when an Open-Bar
All-You-Can-Drink Young-Politicians
Mixer turns ugly, a whole reserved floor
looking like the Baghdad Hilton three years
into the occupation, the pool area completely
trashed after the convention officers were
caught tossing flutes by the case at the pool,
not caring whether the glasses missed or not.
They pay an undertrained, overworked staff
jack shit and then hold them responsible
when anything goes wrong while they're
exercising their managerial prerogative
to bang the head waitress, hostess, night auditor
in comp suites, wasted on the personal stock
bought and paid for by the company but never
invoiced, inventoried or accounted for.
They crack on the wait staff for not selling
enough drinks but turn a blind eye to
the weekend hookers turning tables in
the lounge four maybe five times a night; and
are overheard saying, "They pay for the best
rooms, top dollar on drinks. Who cares what
they do on their own time." Don't mention
the kickbacks or the pieces of pie on the side
that come as some of the unstated perks of
the job. They insist you'll never move up
in the organization, aren't really managerial
timber, if you question authority or refuse
to play ball which is fine with you. The only
team sport you're interested in is baseball,
looking forward to the day you will burn your
resume in the lobby and piss on the ashes.

**Alan Catlin**

## Fire Mare

I have driven this road twice a week
      since September, passing this field
first on my left, then to my right,
         returning.  I have glanced with half
a mind at the acre of fading grasses,
       noticed the vague shape of a horse, grazing.

This terrain is like much of any life:
      a tangent, perimeter of thought, not wholly
present, not my field.

Today, as I turn, heading east around the
       curve, I am shocked into vision.  The rain
has stopped and a slow sun has chosen
         this ordinary scene.  A sorrel mare stands
by the fence in halo, each hair of her
       coppery coat illuminated, a precise shining,
         an equine star.

I cannot look away.  She owns this moment
      as though I have never seen a horse before,
never acknowledged what the torched grace of winter
       can do to the soul.

But there are cars behind me and my next
      patient waits.  I drive on, straining in the
rear-view mirror for one more glimpse of brilliance

but see only silhouette: the dark horse,
     the empty shape
       of what we hope to know.

**Joanne Riley Clarkson**

## The Sin Not Taken

I confess that I have never had sex
    in the backseat of a car.  Shy, studious
girl in high school, only child of a widowed
    Catholic mother who taught
        at the parochial school,

I was many years past college, children,
    divorce, before I used the "F" word,
dyed my hair and stood on the curb
        with a protest sign.

And now, between arthritis and stretch
    marks, The Backseat is honestly
        one of those things it is too late for
doing but not imagining:

The late spring night, face of the awkward
    lover mimed with moon-, star- and distant city-
lights.  Rolling and ripping the shoplifted
    panties.  Climbing over the seats
into the back, fabric cool and stiff beneath me.
    Smells of oil and candy wrappers.  Shine
of an empty soda can

as the bra unsnaps and breasts, like small, sweet
    blushing mushrooms,
        hunger for the heat.

Loving the sin more than the man-boy's
    tongue.  Breath traveling faster than any
road race. Windows turning to cloud
        as I kneel on air and feel inside me
        everything but shame.

And if I could live one day of my life over,
    on a Friday afternoon in mid-May,
I would tap that boy with reddish wavy hair,
    the one who sat in front of me in math class,
also studious and shy.

I would tap him on the shoulder and whisper:
    "Your backseat or mine?"

**Joanne Riley Clarkson**

## Micronauts

When I was young as my microscope
I wanted to become the first man
on the atom.  Why go to Mars when
you can visit the strange heavens inside
a leaf,
a salt grain,
or some anonymous slide of pond water.
Leave Andromeda and the one filling
her ladle with meteorites
to someone else.
I'd be happy to become a micronaut,
colonize star-systems I could
carry on the tip of a pencil.

Maybe atoms are really planets, tiny earthspheres
scattered with cities,
electrons shining like moons in the night sky.
And the inhabitants–
are they as strong as any
of the monsters I dreamed while growing up,
or are they like us, only
shorter and with an extra toe.

Even as I speak
galaxies are growing inside me
large as Mohican Road, smaller
than the DNA I lost inside a mosquito.

And though my microscope is gone
I still think there's a man
like myself on one of those worlds,
he and his life-mate wishing upon
molecules and the lights of mitochondria
that shiver in the blackness
over the farside mountains.

Rob Cook

## Alphabet Stupor

A was away.
B was barely there.
C had simply collapsed
into a swaybacked chair, while
dutiful D did dishes, mumbling.
E eyed F, who eponymously swore
at G & H, that ghastly pair, stumbling
over bodies on their way out the door.

Night before, I had invited the gang,
plus DJ & his combo Special K,
the belle known as L (at least for today)
and the M & M twins–at shebangs
like this, they melt in your hand.
N swung in late, toting nips of his own.
O, that band, they partied full-strength,
'til at arm's length, P passed the phone–
*QUIET!* squawked the 2-Q tenant,
as 3-R rattled the pipes in a riot act.
But S sang out to timid T, *U can't*
*stop now, man!* Big V & W
backed out in their belching van.
*Kiss me,* pled X in exhausted air,
then keeled over on the spot.
Best not to ask Y. Elsewhere,
Z was last seen at the zoo,
gazing at A in a
rendezvous.

**Barbara Lydecker Crane**

**Hello, Out There . . .**

The phone continues to ring.

I pick up the receiver.
It's someone I don't know
calling from a bar.  It's a wrong number.
Loud music.  Bar sounds.
"Listen," a drunken voice says.
"Rick done some bad shit last night.
And we had to tie him down.
Do you want to talk to him?"

"Sure," I say.

He came on the line.  He calls me Ernie.
"Is that you, Uncle Ernie?"

"Yeah," I lie in a slack-jawed response.

"I did some bad shit, Uncle Ernie.
I broke a bunch of windows out.
And I hurt some people."
"Do me a favor," I say.
"Okay, Uncle Ernie.
What do you want me to do?"
"Who called me?"
"Cousin Jack."
"Can you reach him?"
"Yeah, I could . . . ."

"I want you to reach over
and slug Jack in the face."
"Really?"
"Absolutely right.  Harder'n
you've ever hit anyone
in your life."
"Why?"
"Don't ask,
just do it, NOW."
"Okay."
I hear a thud.
A "Son of a Bitch."
And then, the sound of
things breaking.

**Steve De France**

## Ditch

I wade the inlay of stagnant rain between field and
    Jappa Road.  Cattail and reeds sway, shad
    and lamb's ear startle then blanch.  More exotic
    these milkweed pods at sundown than Hong Kong
    to me who has never been anywhere.
I dust the corrugated pipe for dragonflies to light on
    and toads to croak on, no lust for Prague when
    I sit in the mutter and chatter of beetles and
    ladybugs, horseflies and gnats, the foursquare
    congregation of monarch butterflies.
I want to breathe all this into my body–the potato moth's
    white panting, the waving of Queen Anne's Lace,
    golden rod spewing tiny meteorites of seed.
    Mud gives off the odor of rutting, stews the pungent meat
    of a skunk, loosens the lilies from their trumpets.
I belong to this wildness that holds back the shackled,
    cultivation, fields, weeded and pristine.  Paris, Berlin,
    Tokyo, Rio, Chicxulub ripen with fewer delights
    than these thrush nests, this untrampled slather.
Furrows press against the fence, waiting to be plowed
    to the road, but I will not let greed come.
    I stand firm in the oozing rushes and tadpoles
    as the moon floats up.  I name this holy ground.

**Stephanie Dickinson**

## Iowa

Farm girls undress, swim in the pond like nymphs, float on the brown shimmering water where cows drink. Diving into the muck, they imagine themselves the huntress Artemis, or Aphrodite, born of castrated genitals and the froth of the sea, though they've never seen an ocean or mountain. They've been dropped from the thigh of Zeus, these two with chore buckets, pulling their overalls back on, girls hoping to bloom in one sultry corn-weather afternoon. I remember my best friend. Wild, never praised, brazen, Linda had a father who worked her like a son, and even after our swims, she smelled of the hog wallows. We walked barefoot into the sweetness of dusk that had been forever coming. Bangs hanging in our eyes, we were three miles south of anywhere, daubing our farmer-tanned wrists with Ben Hur. No escape from the hayfields ripening on every side, from the orange trumpets of ditch lilies following us. My cousin, bespectacled and freckled, trotted his pony alongside. *I could never love you,* she shooed him. She wanted red Mustangs, Harley Davidsons, anything fast to take her away. Crickets whirled as we cut into the cemetery. We wandered over the graves, talked to the blue-eyed upper classman, Jack Holub, killed in a tractor accident. We sat on my father's cracked headstone. *I wish we could trade,* she'd say, already breasty, milkiness pushing out the bib of her coveralls. No town boy would find us though we were goddesses. Splitting a can of warm Falstaff, we were frantic for forbidden fruit. But this was Iowa, black-soil country, and dangerousness came slower than the glaciers. Her father, wearing waders and hard looks, was quicker. Already looking for us.

**Stephanie Dickinson**

**Second Base on the Banana Boat**

So hard to make a double play
in this humidity.  The air is soft
and wobbly.  At the height of the pivot,

the Amazon with all its piranhas
slides under me, tries to take me out.
A tarantula from the banana pile

waits in the on-deck circle, spitting
on his feelers and rubbing them briskly
together before picking up a bat.

Foul balls bounce off the jungle
canopy, unravel into the air
like a flutter of albino parrots.

A *tour de force* is slithering on first,
staring me down with a crocodile smile.
The hit-and-run is on.  The anaconda

in the box seats is growing larger
and larger as the entire front row
disappears one at a time.  I cheat

a step or two towards first to cover
the hole.  The sky lobs a quick
monsoon at us.  The infield draws

the twitching tarpaulin over itself.
We outrun typhoid to the dugout and relax,
drenching our sweaty faces in mosquitoes.

**James Doyle**

**Watching you sleep . . .**

is like snorkeling
in tropical waters.

I am entranced by the shifts
in the light and form of your face.

Bold and weightless, I explore
the translucence that surrounds:

soft coral fingers
peek out from a cave,

elongated ribbon reefs
pile and fall around your head,

angel fish flash softly
in your dark eye spaces,

a sponge swells and shrinks
in the shape of your nose,

an open clam, giant, red-lined,
has taken the place of your mouth,

sea grass at your temples
drifts and hides small creatures,

sea urchins cluster
around your cheeks and chin.

Your belly on the seabed,
your face chin-down on the pillow –

you are a green turtle in repose;
an outstanding example

representing the major stages
in Earth's evolutionary history,

the ongoing ecological process
of a superlative natural phenomenon.

I am careful how I touch.
I must remember how to breathe.

**Nicola Easthope**

## Lay the Sod o'er Me

We made his coffin out of soft, white pine,
long boards for the sides scored to bend
into wide-shouldered contours of the old shape.
Lines of grain accented
knots of deep-earth brown
like eyes of the old pine looking out to its utility.
It had holes in the bottom for the ground
to join him when the snows melt to run-off.

We burned, on the top, the horizon silhouette
of the mountain he could see from his bed,
and sheep on the range,
and an old sheep wagon with off-center door
like the one he called home as a boy.

On the end board we burned a leaping trout
about to grab at the hand-tied fly on his line;
on the sides, rough designs
of all the wildlife of his wild life.

For handles we picked six horseshoes
from an old oil bucket behind the barn—
rusted, worn, encrusted in the grooves
with manure and mountain mud.
We screwed them into strips of cowhide
marked with his brand—*lazy M, inverted T, bar*—
fastened to the coffin, three on a side.

And for planting him down
like a seed into new-ploughed ground,
we used lassos,
three of them, each at least fifteen feet.
Six ranch-hands
at the sides of the hole
slowly unwound the ropes.

**Maureen Tolman Flannery**

30

**Two Step**

Hartford, '43. The big-band clubs swing
with doomed youths, sucking nightlife
into their wartime daze.

He is another soldier on furlough who
cuts in, out, as always, for a good time.
She is a key punch operator at the Aetna.

She wears high platforms that pump
music into the curve of her calves.
She will confess to me, positioning

Dr. Scholls' squashed donut pads
over her corns, that her youthful vanity,
via those shoes, ruined her dancing feet.

He is a handsome cowboy who can dance.
What chance does she have?
He has two-stepped her out of the canteen

and onto her porch cot. She is not,
nor will she ever be, the only thing
on his mind, as he is hers.

The couch, white wicker with the weave
frayed, sends reed shoots in odd directions
like vine tendrils feeling for something rooted

to grab onto. The chenille spread,
draped across the back, covers them
from the night's chill as my mother,

with dark wavy hair and large coquettish eyes
that contradict her prudish piety, trades
the ruby of her wholeness for a pirate's chest

of longing buried in wet sand of her aspirations.
She has invited the future in, and it is hard
and unresponsive as this cot,

and yet, expectant as she soon will be.
They have not yet learned that charm
does not discriminate among recipients.

They do not know where the clarity
of her flashing eyes will go when
disappointment drops a dark scrim before them.

They are four years and half a continent
away from my birth. She carries my potency
in a pouch at her side like a gold doubloon.

My sister will join them soon.  I am
waiting until they are surrounded by wood—
log cabin walls with pine forest outside.

I cannot be enticed into city matter
even by his charm
or the dark, flirty flash of her Irish eyes.

**Maureen Tolman Flannery**

## Mittens

we wear mittens to protect our hands from each other there are no fingers entwined in this relationship. we wear big jackets like puffed up penguins struggling to walk struggling to keep the cold out but it's not just the air that is frozen solid our breath visible spreading before our faces in the dark night with the stars drowning disappearing in all that sky when we should be alone and safe and apart. there's no one on these streets we walk alone and jagged to find your house your kitchen your fridge with the photo of your ex still on it buried under magnets but it's still there. we've moved on from beer to tequila to gin and tonic to watered scotch burning our throats to create some artificial warmth swaying tearing coughing through what's left of the night. your cat peppered black white purring or is it growling I can't tell it doesn't seem to know either. I know you but I don't and you don't and you know me but we don't know each other like this. not like this with the lamp still burning even though it's now daytime and the sun has no heat but the lamp burns my fingers when I touch it it's been on all night and you finish the scotch no grimace no burning no pain. no pain for me either this isn't the movies there's no love story here. there's not any kind of story here now that the night has filtered out and spread through. there's no love story here. I promise.

**Christine Fotis**

## Insatiable

I once dreamt that in one night I called up
the assorted sausages of my past, heartily humped
them all in a row. First, I visited Gorilla Face, the man
with the Cro-Magnon size jaw who did sit ups before
bed. As he snored in the sheets, I ran to a pay phone,
got Ultra-Religious Jewish Boy to pick me up for some
thigh-quivering pleasing, then had private cum parties
with Ex Fat Guy, Farm Boy and Valentine's Day Killer.

You trailed me in a Buick Skylark, made the pay phone
cackle like a rooster. I ran away before you caught me
slamming down on a stranger, tracing the socket of his lips,
clutching the granite slab of his shoulder. I was a bad
woman feeling good, following the savage beats of my hips
from bedroom to brick wall to bathroom tile. I ran
and ran, before you could witness me pound our love
into a pulp with the steady rock of my rear.

It had been going too well between us. I'd woken up
too many mornings in the crook of your arm
feeling delicious. My unconscious wanted to sledgehammer
our glass coffee table with every pelvic thrust, every squeeze
of bun, every fevered lick of tongue. I wasn't a nice, Jewish girl
living with you in sin, forwarding my phone so mother
didn't discover I wasn't roommates anymore
with pigtailed Lana, her bed piled with stuffed animal kitties.

I woke up crying and confessed. *Come back to bed.*
*It's OK,* you said. You laughed, admitted that last night
your unconscious had fucked your German ex-girlfriend
in a place called Buttock, Malaysia. *Come back to bed,*
you said, embracing my undeserving inner whore.
You spooned all of me into your warm flesh,
even the part determined to desecrate
before someone stole you away from me first.

**Marilyn Friedman**

34

## Even the Nails in the Sheet Rock Missed Her

When she entered a room, the room paid attention.
When she entered his house,
the leather couches plumped up and shone,
the hardwood floors were giddy with tapping
against the soles of her small black shoes,
the books on the shelves jostled each other
for a better view of the waves of her hair.

When she didn't come, the walls held their breath,
straining to hear her voice, her laugh.
When she still didn't come, that crying noise wasn't him.
The white gauze curtains hung keening,
as they remembered the stroke of her fingers.
And at night, when he turned and turned,
it was only because the bed prodded him continually,
as the pillows pleaded in his ear, "Bring her back."
And when he sat up, his hand on his chest,
how could he breathe,
when all the air had gone out into the street
calling her name?

**Cheryl Gatling**

## For the Woman Who Walked out During My Reading

To what should I attribute it,
an upsurge in sunspot activity

or the general decay of manners?
Please don't say it was me,

the dull sincerity of my words,
their untreated depression,

that sent you rushing off.
Let me think there was a man

(with a ponytail, perhaps),
a vase of dried wildflowers,

a bedroom wall on which
you put a hand for balance

as you stepped out of your skirt,
your micro panties, and then yourself

and delicately into a love poem.

**Howard Good**

## Visit from My Mother on My Birthday

*June 27, Andros Island, Greece*

My mother sits on the ledge
of my balcony
overlooking the pool
and the Aegean Sea.

She blocks my view of
the island's geraniums,
bougainvillea and
beach umbrellas.
She says she bleached
the sheets on my hotel bed
and scoured the sink
with Borax and Bon Ami.

My friend Barbara,
the psychoanalyst,
says it takes more than
a breath to get over
a mother's death.
My daughter Liz
says I have a vivid
imagination.

But I swear, there is my mother
in a Swirl housedress, 40's wedgies,
her rimless glasses perched
on her nose like mine.

"Why are you here?" I ask
as the ferry to Tinos
sticks its nose out
of the rocky cliffs
and sails silently across
my page.

"It's your birthday, right?" She winks.
"Birthing you was like God
building Andros Island,
pushing it up and
out of the sea. No small thing!"
"Go back to Brooklyn," I beg.
"You don't belong here among
Greek ruins and broiled octopus."

My mother is indifferent
to ferry schedules or
broken ancient pottery.
She doesn't want to climb
the steps to the Acropolis,
or say the names
Dionysus, Aphrodite or Apollo.

Instead she gazes at
a boy in an orange
bathing suit climbing
out of the hotel pool.

I write the words:
*boy in an orange bathing suit,*

and she is gone.

**June S. Gould**

## A Frat Guy on a Motorcycle

Regardless of what I thought
of his baseball hat turned backwards
and the hundred-dollar Ray-Ban shades;

or the severed sleeves of his T-shirt
and the tribal band tattoo winding his bicep;

or the girl—Good Lord, that beautiful girl
strapped tail-up behind him on the Kawasaki—
in tiny denim shorts, two long gulps
of golden leg straddling the hot engine.

Regardless of my opinions,
my simple and stubborn stereotyping,
I envied the look on this man's tanned face
when he stopped at a red light beside me.

It was a look that said, in no uncertain terms,
*My life is good right now. Yes. Damn good.*

**Nathan Graziano**

## Two Girls in a Tub Together

Maybe you're hoping for a supermodel
to slip out of a slinky red dress,
kick off a pair of stiletto pumps,
and step lightly onto a cold, tiled floor.
A few feet away another woman
will wait with parted lips in a Roman tub,
steam rising from the still water.
The two beauties will then embrace,
their breasts lathered with bubbles,
their smooth, shaved legs entangled
as their pink tongues flicker like moths.

So it might come as a disappointment
when I tell you that the two girls in the tub
are my wife and eighteen-month-old daughter.
They're splashing and laughing,
having fun as clean as a yellow rubber duck.

I'm in the other room listening to them,
a bit choked up by my love for both.
I fold my hands over my stomach and smile,
as astounded as you by my own caprices.

Nathan Graziano

## Thanksgiving at Jill's House

It was a different kind of law
and he, an atypical judge.
But the dining room table
was unquestionably a court
and, sat before knives, forks
and spoons, was a wide range
of defendants.

But it was a church too.
It wasn't God exactly
who sat at table's head
but an errant cough would set
those heavy eyes to rolling heavenward
in hopes the trinity could stand to be a foursome.

It was an army as well.
Brothers on either side
were foot soldiers
though it were hands
that nervously reached across the
table's grim frontier.

And it was an office of the severest kind,
where the only humor
stems from boss's bon mots,
and no woman yet
had breached that
thick glass ceiling
of having an opinion.

It was family but not
the kind that I was used to.
He said Grace.
He sliced the fowl.
But not the tough charred atmosphere.

And it was a prison camp.
Jill risked the commandant's wrath
by occasionally escaping to my glance.
But how much tunnel can you dig
with half a smile.

**John Grey**

## The Last Photograph of My Father

My daughter is in his lap
like a bouquet of flowers.
Like the bouquet that would
come to the door from a friend
three days later.
But that is not the miracle.
The miracle is my mother
who appeared uninvited,
who walked across the room,
and stood by his chair, though no one
would have asked her to do this.
Not because she did not belong,
but my mother refuses to be in pictures,
turns her head, covers her face, scowls.
Even on a wedding photograph she waves
an angry arm at the photographer.
In a teenage photo she tries to strangle
her kid brother with the camera.
So no one asks my mother to be in pictures.
This photo was to be of my daughter and father,
but my mother got up
and crossed the room unbidden,
positioned herself in the center behind him
and though unpracticed, she smiled,
as if she knew she belonged there,
as if she heard his heart
counting down.

**Rasma Haidri**

## White Hole

The elderly poet, famous for prizes and privacy,
walked quickly and quietly into the bookstore
straight up to the shelf of New Titles.
He looked first to his left, then to his right,
and, sure he hadn't been recognized,
he took down a heavy anthology.
The pages fell open on his very chapter.
There was his name and his picture too –
the one which his late wife had taken
and which he had made the publisher use
despite its being decades too young.
There was the blurb of his bio and titles
which had been written by his agent's intern.
And there, of course, were six of his poems.
Two he could recite by heart
from God-knows-how-many readings,
and one which he thought he'd lost years ago
and which he insisted be included.
For the other three he still had doubts
about their selection and order.
He followed each line of verse with his finger,
silently mouthing the words. But, as he read,
he found himself glancing up the page at his name
and at the parentheses beneath it.
It gave a year, a dash, and a space
(like a little hole, he thought) waiting to be filled.
Again and again it drew his attention
until it fixed both his finger and eye.
Then, as he stared, it seemed to him
that his bio blurb began to melt, dissolving into
a puddle of ink. And, pulled by some strange gravity,
it flowed up the page and poured itself
into the little white hole. His picture was next,
crumbling like a sheet of spring ice making
a creek of colored water tumbling into the hole.
The little white hole seemed to be growing.
His poems began to yield to its pull, till line by line
like an anchor chain with its hawser cut,
they rattled into the bottomless thing.
And still the white hole grew larger and stronger.
His hat was next, and then his cane,
his tie and shirt, his pants and shoes.
At the loss of his socks he was nearly upended.
His left hand clutched at the band of his shorts
while his right hand tried to close the book.
But the strain was too much for the cheap cotton cloth.
With a rip they flew off and into the hole.
All of the bookstore's customers and clerks
were looking at him. The elderly poet, so famous
for prizing his privacy, was public now as never before.

He knew there was only one place to hide.  One snatch
in vain for his glasses, and he gave his body to gravity.
He disappeared down the waiting hole.
The big gleaming book fell to the floor.
And the cover slammed shut behind him.

**Joseph Hart**

Loons

One rainy late-summer afternoon in Maine
my father and I took a sauna together
in the woods, by ourselves;
then we swam in the cold lake,
too far out for me; my father just kept on
swimming. I followed. There was mist across the lake,
and I worried that he might disappear, that I might forget
the direction to shore. And then, just as I called out
that I couldn't keep up, that I was turning back,
we swam up against a huge rock, almost
an island, submerged just beneath the surface.
We pulled ourselves out and surveyed the mist
over the water: We couldn't see the shore
or hear anything but our own bodies. The rain
had stopped. We stood there breathing, naked,
when my father started talking, hesitantly
at first, about loons, about their mournful songs,
about how rare they are, how rarely they allow
any human to see them. They mate for life,
he said. Then he told me other things I wish
I could remember, and then he kissed me
between my shoulder blades, sat down on the edge
of that rock so only his shoulders and head
were above the water—while I stood, a skinny boy,
beside him—and then he pushed off from that sitting
position, slipped into the water, and swam
back with his sure stroke, stopping only once
to gesture to me to follow.
That night I slept on the screened porch, inside
the exuberant, billion-throated calls of just-born
frogs, inside the scribble of fireflies,
the echo of owl-hoot, silence, and the mournful
calls—way out in the mist—of loons,
which kept me awake, though I tried not to listen.

Michael Hettich

**This Love**

My love is not that of mythical motorbike trips
to fragile Florence
at eighteen years of age.
Of hot hotel bedrooms
covered with petals peeled
from the safe summer rose.
Not that which Bronte bore on the moors.
Nor that of doomed Paris
watching his bold brother die.
A simple sacrifice
to the patchwork passion of his love.

But not equally of Theseus,
I have no ship to sail away.
Not that of shining silver words
rusting in the rain
that wild winter brings.
Of love pledged forever
on the polished bathroom floor,
snatched savage back
in the passenger seat of a small second-hand car
parked by the shore
overlooking the river
as it flows to Cobh.
I won't cross the moors,
one house for another.

They will call me a child,
lovesick prepubescent,
for these honey words,
but fuck them.
Mine is a small love
of ham-salad sandwiches,
dinners made and cups of tea.
The kind you never find in odes and elegies.
Of children playing
when I am old.
I'll look into your eyes then
and show you all.
This is the love I have for you.
Take it,
if it is enough.

**Kenneth Hickey**

## The Day Everybody Went on Strike

Maybe it started when the garbage grew mountain high
and the pilots left their planes and
clerks refused to sell.  Maybe it started
when one baby refused to take its bottle
or a child boycotted its bath.

Maybe it began that way, but it spread
from people to things.  Refrigerators
refused to keep things cold; cars
locked their wheels and would not move;
doors bickered with their hinges
and would not open; matches could be hit
with hammers and still not light.

Maybe flies from the mountain ranges
of garbage carried the virus.  By noon
no machines would move even if you bribed
them with vintage oil.  Then it got worse.
The tide solidified in mid retreat; wind
took a rest.  No bird flew; no fish swam.

Then it really got bad:  hearts not pumping,
lungs not breathing.  The sun welded itself
to a spot in the sky.  Everywhere nothing
was doing what it was meant to do.
Ears refused to hear all that silence;
eyes refused to report all that lack of motion.
The last clock stopped swinging its hands
at 2:15, and it was 2:15 forever.

**Robert Hoeft**

## The Departure

"What are you doing?"

He stood slouched in the doorway.
She finished folding her skirt,
put it in her suitcase, snicked
the latches shut—click—click.
It was an hour before dinner;
nothing roasted in the oven.
She checked her watch.
In five minutes, if it was on time,
the space ship would arrive.

She looked at him and smiled,
looked around the bedroom
as if it were an exhibit
in a museum she hadn't wanted to visit,
looked out the window
to the garden she wouldn't harvest,
looked back at him and smiled.

He followed her to the front door,
blinked stupidly when the cab horn beeped,
didn't even try to stop her as she brushed past.
His mouth was open like a fruit jar
as she pulled away not even waving.
She would call later, ask, "What are you doing?"
then hang up.  She would do it every day
maybe for years.  Until she was even.

**Robert Hoeft**

## Chromolinguistics

*Language to ashes*
*Text to dust*
*Our land's first artist*
*is laid to rest.*

from *Elegy* (c. 5000 BCE)

The ghost is in the ground,
the ghost is in the cave,
the ghost has dots & lines,
the ghost vibrates in humid cave-wall paintings,
the ghost is the paintings,
the ghost is cubist & ancient,
& I am the ancient cubist painting's final patron,
a viewer misplaced (detached temporally), an idea, a body,
an *e pluribus unum* of ideas,
but I, Lucius Fibonacci, a separate mind, a line drawer, will be cubist,
& I will hear the cosmic background radiation's pre-luminescence,
& I will anticipate enlightenment's melodic spheres,
& I will paint on the eternal backdrop of cave walls

an entrance & an egress.

.

At the cave's infinitesimal end:
a pre-Luminescent, with one vision & one song, paints—
the pre-Luminescent is a being who, with paintbrushes, sticks, moss lamps, & thighs,
   alchemizes this cave
by painting with hemoglobin drawn from my thigh,
is a being with sagging breasts & a cosmology on its ass,
is a being that is an uncelebrated ghost who is unable to celebrate.

I turn & cave moisture reflects my facial capillaries.
I strum a stalactite
& sing my sixteenth-note understanding of pre-neo-cubism & my paintbrush cognizance
   of the cave.
I attempt to see through my monochromaticism.
I see zigzags & dots, I scream,
I'm hypnotized, my flesh trembles, my heart beats 5/4 time, I salivate.

I am in a theatre with stiff-muscled patron-viewers in raincoats & no popcorn.
Am I a projector?
I laugh out, "Where am I cast on the screen?" to the dead guy next to me, anyone near,
   you, reader, "Are you a Neo-Luminescent? a projection?"
"Quiet, unless you paint me to be."
"Are you the dots & lines?"
"Are dimensions necessary," you reply through the page,
& if I say, "No," will I become a pointillist.

.

I crave a cubist perspective to investigate
all the cave's hollows, all the stalactites of resonance,
the stalagmite of now, the perspective, the now-angle, a neo-now angle.
& a Thing & a Self, & a Thing-in-a-Self that is nothing.
Thing that stands, that is cast; Self that speaks, that has chromatic grammar: that is
    myriad Thing-in-Self,
but that is not my projection,
that is not my drawing,
that is not my vowels, nor consonants,
but, nonetheless, heeds my vowels!

The Thing is a cage cast by reverends of the Iron.
Horizontal & vertical monochrome bars welded, a cosmic lattice
between me & the prism of perspectives—
polychromatic blasts from cosmic background radiation.
The iron bars' intersections alchemize radiation to sounds & colors.
The cage is the Idea—
the awakened cubist cave element,
lines spiraled thru time to the viewer,
its own idea revealed in detail, at last,
again & again, into quantum levels with constant chaos continually calculated,
& the concept of its own detail.

The Idea recreates the cave from pre-caved times.  Thus,
it might be a hydrogen atom or an Aleph dragging permuted ions created from
    vowels bouncing around the cave in exact echo of initial announcement—
voicing a grander idea of the cave
& expanding perspectives thru a universe & immense cosmologies.
It might be a golden rectangle drawn on one ghost mind
or a reflection of the uncelebrated ghost mind.
It might be poems from a Neo-Luminescent,
or a reflection of my mind, perhaps in my mind,
perhaps in the mind that wrote this poem,
or the poem's own mind that thinks the Thing that is the beginning & the end.

& perhaps the mind will die.

The ghost, the songless, the prayerless, the secret-from-us, the unhypothesized limitless,
    the being who creates being,
who exhilarates in quantum detail, perceives thru all dimensions in multiple-
    perspectives simultaneously—multiple & single act uniquely,
& am I unable to appreciate?

•

I, Lucius Fibonacci, hypothesize a ghost-idea,
& I hypothesize the ghost:
the ghost dwells in the underground,
the ghost is humid like the cave,
the ghost dwells in the cave walls,
the ghost invades the unawake,

the ghost will fade into the wall with the paint,
the ghost will appear from the wall,
the ghost paints itself,
the ghost is poly-rhythmic,
the ghost flies like desire made song,
the ghost screams of death in ghost-consonants,
the cry of birth is ghost-vowels,
the ghost is in the tomb,
& the ghost is in the womb,
the ghost is unique to itself uniquely,
I need the ghost to inspire me to be lyric, polychromatic,
the ghost thinks like the alphabet,
the ghost speaks from all times,
the ghost always hears itself,
the ghosts needs to sleep,
the ghost needs to rest from multi-perspectives,
the ghost needs to be repainted by a neo-now-painter,
the ghost needs me,
the ghost invites me with colors,
the ghost invites me with brush,
the ghost gives me endless canvas
& the awakeness to be apart from awakeness, to perceive.
The ghost calls me to wake & sleep, to sing,
I sleep, I wake, again & again simultaneously.
The ghost can't exist independent of me.
The ghost vibrates in the humid cave-wall paintings.
The ghost whispers a consonant
& sounds a round vowel.

.

Dots & zigzags vortex into the walls,
painted ghosts leap from the walls,
stalactites resonate bass tones,
new colors are alchemized,
eyes envision, perceive,
& one idea in one drawn line on one cave wall becomes multi-idea, multi-color
    perspectives in multi-dimensions painted into the wall,
& becomes energy, becomes consciousness, becomes Idea, becomes vision, & becomes
    the cubism of a Neo-Omnipresent-Luminescent, Lucius Fibonacci—
an awakened ghost-viewer-patron-painter for the eternal palimpsest, the eternal cave
    wall.

**Tom Holmes**

## How You'll Know You've Met Your Future Wife
*for my sons*

One day, a girlfriend will throw you a party. "Surprise!"
All your exes will spring up, like Jills-in-the-boxes,
from behind your furniture. Your girlfriend will explain
that she is leaving you, that she's had it, that she wasn't
sure how to tell you why, so she tracked down all these others,
all your former lovers, to help articulate just what it is
about you that's so irredeemably wrong. "You didn't change
your shirts or the sheets enough," one will shout.
"You remembered the batting averages of all the Red Sox, but
not my birthday," another will say, throwing a lit candle
at you like a fastball. You'll hear about how you were
too gassy, too cheap. One will say you freaked her out
when you whispered in her ear, and another will recall
how she pointed to page 84 in *The Joy of Sex,* how you turned
red, how you turned the page, said no, but maybe page 16,
after some more white wine, and then passed out.
When they finally finish, you'll be torn in pieces
that your exes will fling around the room and stomp on
with high heels, and the better part of you
will pool at the feet of your newest ex-girlfriend.
Just when you're giving up on yourself and on love,
one of your eyes will see someone new, a party crasher
just there to get out of the rain, and to get some cake.
Her eyes will be glassy with tears. She will flick a smile at you
and this will make you strong enough to pull yourself together.
You will notice a large smudge of icing on her nose, but that
won't bother you at all, and you won't dream of telling her.

**Tom C. Hunley**

**Robinson Crusoe**
(the abridged novel as an MP3)

"The Wanderer" (Dion and The Belmonts)
"I'm Moving On" (Rascal Flatts)
"Into the Great Wide Open" (Tom Petty)
"Can't Nobody Hold Me Down" (Puff Daddy)
"Goodbye to You" (Scandal)
"Sailing" (Christopher Cross)
"Stormy Weather" (Billie Holiday)
"I Get Lost" (Eric Clapton)
"Beyond the Sea" (Bobby Darin)
"A Thousand Miles from Nowhere" (Dwight Yoakam)
"Welcome to the Jungle" (Guns 'N' Roses)
"Walk on the Wild Side" (Lou Reed)
"Hot Hot Hot" (Buster Poindexter)
"Sand in My Shoes" (Dido)
"Help!" (The Beatles)
"Rescue Me" (Aretha Franklin)
"Gimme Shelter" (Rolling Stones)
"Hungry Like the Wolf" (Duran Duran)
"I Drink Alone" (George Thorogood)
"Dirty White Boy" (Foreigner)
"I Will Survive" (Gloria Gaynor)
"Through the Years" (Kenny Rogers)
"Christmas in the Caribbean" (Jimmy Buffett)
"So Lonely" (The Police)
"Sometimes You Can't Make It on Your Own" (U2)
"Footprints in the Sand" (George Benson)
"Who Can It Be Now?" (Men at Work)
"Thank God It's Friday" (R. Kelly)
"Hey, Good Looking" (Hank Williams)
"Just What the Doctor Ordered" (Ted Nugent)
"Lonely No More" (Rob Thomas)
"Sharing the Night Together" (Dr. Hook)
"Land of 1000 Dances" (Cannibal and The Headhunters)
"20 Years" (Placebo)
"Homesick" (The Cure)
"Somewhere I Belong" (Linkin Park)
"So Far Away" (Carole King)
"London Calling" (The Clash)
"Let Me Be There" (Olivia Newton John)
"Come Sail Away" (Styx)
"Green Green Grass of Home" (Tom Jones)
"My Happy Ending" (Avril Lavigne)
"Diary" (Bread)

**Lockie Hunter**

## Some Things My Sister Left Behind

One doll with a painted white face and a delicate purple fan that our father brought back from Chinatown (Exxon station bathroom, just outside of Memphis)

One yellow plaid hair ribbon with her name, Aimee, embroidered in purple script (Samuel Jackson playground, Memphis)

Two tonsils (Doctor Simmons office, Memphis)

Three Judy Bloom books (under bunk number seven, cheerleading camp, Nashville)

One trophy, "Best Poem 1976: Samuel Jackson Junior High" (bedside table, bedroom, Memphis)

One retainer (boyfriend's house, Memphis)

One 1980 Toyota Corolla, white with beige interior: totaled (Peabody Service and Towing, Memphis)

One letter from dad encouraging her to "excel in her studies and drive carefully dammit now that you are up there in Yankeeland;" signed "I love you so much, baby." (shoebox under bed, Boston)

Twenty-five assorted love letters from seven different boys dated 1982-2006 (shoebox under bed, Boston)

Five little black dresses (hanging in closet, bedroom, Boston)

Three unpaid speeding tickets (sitting on desk under three-day-old Starbucks mocha latte, home office, Boston)

Two "respectable" business suits, both heather gray (hanging in bedroom closet, Boston)

Two unfed cats sitting on the windowsill, waiting (kitchen, Boston)

Three pairs of blue jeans: two faded Levi's, boot-cut size 7M with butt and knees missing, one Guess slim-fit size-four never worn (bureau, bedroom, Boston)

One unfinished memoir titled "My Life in Words" (C: drive, Dell computer, home office, Boston)

Four pints of blood (Massachusetts Turnpike between Boston and Cambridge)

One recipe for asparagus with pecan brown butter (recipe box, kitchen, Boston)

One 1987 VW bug, sunflower-yellow with cloud-white interior; totaled (Commonwealth Service and Towing, off the Massachusetts Turnpike between Cambridge and Boston)

Nineteen detailed photo albums recording her unfinished life (knotty pine bookshelf, living room, Boston)

One antique wedding gown, circa 1948, found at garage sale (HOPE chest, foot of bed, Boston)

One mother, forty-nine-years-old, deciding between five little black dresses and two "respectable" suits to bring to funeral parlor (bedroom closet, Boston)

One detailed "incident resulting in loss of life" form 192B filed in triplicate (Cambridge Police station, District Six Station, Cambridge)

One sister, twenty-two-years-old, on computer, writing (Memphis)

**Lockie Hunter**

## To What Habit Do You Attribute
## the Longevity of Your Marriage?

So we're having an argument
about politics—most of our thirty
years of marriage we belonged to
different parties—and our car's off
the road, off the crumbling cliff
and into the cumulus and robin's egg
half a mile before we notice
and only then do we plummet.
The parachute of my pink sunbonnet
slows us—down we rock like that tree-top
cradle until an Acme rocket
shoots a hole like a heart and shatters
our target: a bridge over a mad river
complete with whirlpools to hell (see
those red-tailed devils, pitchforks poised
to pop our tires?) when Daffy Duck
lands on our hood.  Despite our warnings
with dingbats aplenty, he dons
a top hat, does a tap dance
(with spats, cane, full orchestration)
which shifts the trajectory
of our Chevy to the six lanes
of mayhem and we try to recall
whose turn it was to pay the car
insurance, the life insurance, and
boing! here we are on a shiny
Acme mattress truck.  We have a big
face-sucking kiss so we don't notice
the dark tunnel—oh, suffering
succotash, heavens to murgatroid—
that sloughs us off to a desert
where we hang on matching arms
of a cactus and vultures discuss
the proper spices for such aged
specimens when, as you expected,
the Roadrunner beeps and Coyote's
pinwheel legs spin up enough
turbulence to blow the birds off
screen and us back to this couch,
watching Saturday morning TV.

Marcia L. Hurlow

## Big Daddy

Called me Hot Stuff.  Called me Ragtop,
Lugnut, your Deere-in-the-Driveway Duchess.

Called forth Bad Company from the pickup's stereo
and, lo, I appeared with a buck knife

and a hundred-proof smile, my battered hunter's manual
tucked in the waistband of my cutoffs.

What were we at first but two necks of the same guitar,
high on the blister of our power riff?  Each night

was a stadium tour, each day an album cover
fit for collecting.  How precious,

how practiced we looked those weekends at the lake,
posing in our matching hipwaders and stabbing

at the world's swamp-stink with the gig of our love.
But forever is a black fish hiding in cattails, a fat plop

always sounding out of range.  Soon, the lake iced over.
The far-off smoke of forest fires stole your attention.

While I dreamt pyrotechnics for our stage duets,
you and your matchbox slid out the window.

No note.  No final mix tape.  No rose left thorny
on the nightstand.  I searched for you in parking lots

until a passing trucker said he'd caught your show
in Denver, that you wore a silk shirt and played everything

acoustic, and the news rocked me like a last-track ballad.
Oh Big Daddy, Daddy with the Long Legs,

father of a stillborn promise and my liveliest rage,
for weeks I choked on your name, stuck so deep

in my craw it took a crowbar and two months
of keg stands in Assumption, Illinois, to dislodge it.

Now, I drink sweet tea in a Southern state.  Now,
I am patient.  Here, small likenesses of you croak to me

from their lilypadded thrones.  I'd like to mistake
their bellows for green apologies, but I know better.

At night, I hunt them with a three prong.  I fry them
in batter and grease.  We both know what they taste like.

**Carrie Jerrell**

57

## Plainsong

If you saw my footprints around the barn loft's ladder,
you would know I tie each bale with sisal twine and secrets.

If you saw me kneel among cut sweetcorn stalks,
you would know I hear vespers in the auger's rush.

If Red-tails scouted the warren's edge, or murders called
from their barbed-wire roosts, you would hide me in rows
of ruby snapdragons, mend my briar-lashed hands;

like the dobbin, you would carry me where jack-in-the-pulpits grow
beneath cathedraling white oak and hickory.

If sunset turned ripe wheatfields honey-gold,
and the combine hummed as it cleared the hundredth acre;
if, after dark, haze hung like a new heaven above the furrows,

you would know the harvest moon is near,
that sheets left on the line will smell of blazing stars in the morning,

and that I wait upstairs for you, barefoot on the pine floor,
unplaiting the amber linens of my hair.

**Carrie Jerrell**

## Mall of America

To get here by one, leave by 12:30.
Take Washington past the Mobil station, the public library,
Kinko's, Gold's Gym, Target, and on the corner
of State and Washington you'll see Dunkin' Donuts,
Office Max and TGI Friday's.
Turn left at the light.
Drive about a half-mile.
On your left'll be Lowe's, Wendy's, Best Buy,
Pep Boys, and Pet Supermarket.
On your right'll be Burger King, Radio Shack, Home Depot,
Petco, and Auto Nation.
The next light is Main.
Make a left.
You'll pass Starbucks, McDonald's, Subway, Wal-Mart,
Sports Authority, Bank of America, Einstein Bagels,
Blockbuster Video, a Shell station, and the first Fifth Third Bank.
Make another left at the intersection of Main and Church.
You'll pass the massive AMC movie theatre, Arby's,
Balley's Total Fitness, Denny's, and the UPS Store.
The mall will be on your left: Benningan's, Macy's, Lord and Taylor,
Sears, Sears Auto, Nordstrom, Cheesecake Factory, Citibank.
Go over the highway and make the third left onto Second Ave.
If you get out to the dealerships
—Honda, Toyota, Saab, Volvo, Volkswagon—you've gone too far.
On Second, make a U-turn at the first stop sign,
cut through the BP parking lot
and make a left back onto Church.
Borders Books will be on your right,
Barnes & Noble across the street.
Past Borders is Oak Street,
which looks like an alley and will take you behind
the Marriot, past the K-Mart, Comp USA, Papa John's,
another Shell, Starbucks, McDonald's, Blockbuster Video,
and the second Fifth Third Bank.
Turn left onto Maple Ave.
The third stop sign is Hill Street.
Make a right.
My house is the eleventh house on the left.
Don't worry about bringing anything.
We've got plenty of fireworks
and I found a place selling flags three for a dollar.

**Brad Johnson**

## Married Saturday Mornings

I don't want to let you out of bed this Saturday morning.
While a storm lifts the curtains of the open windows
and whiffs of rain sweep through the sliding glass door,
I don't want to roll over, don't want you to sit up,
don't want the telephone to ring or you to dial
because then I will have lost you to your friend
in Happy Valley who's getting married to a Methodist
archeologist from Missouri, or to your other friend
who's getting married outside of New Haven one
week from yesterday and the dresses don't
fit. The best man's threatening to not show. The last
wedding we attended, in Michigan two weeks ago,
was my Irish-Scottish friend's and I wore a kilt and long
wool stockings and no underwear and a little satchel
around my waist where I kept a flask filled
with whiskey. We've been married one month
and I don't want to let you out of bed this Saturday
morning. I've heard if you put a marble in a jar
for every time you have sex during the first year
of marriage and remove one marble for each
time you have sex anytime after, you'll never empty
the jar. I want to fill that jar and empty that jar, construct
new jars, and smooth virgin marbles all weekend.
The storm's raising the curtains higher now, bringing
with it the feeling of trying to grip greased marbles
and other moods I can't yet express about married Saturdays.

**Brad Johnson**

## The Wake

The buffet table is piled
with salads—tuna salad,
macaroni salad, chicken salad,
garden salad, fruit salad.
Melon ballers, olive pickers,
and lemon zesters lay about
the table like forgotten relatives
waiting for rides.  The cold
cuts and antipasto are rolled
like logs waiting to burn
beneath the fire of color of the late-
to-arrive bouquet.  Purple-printed
vines wind round on the napkins;
overcoats stack upon each other
like a gang tackle on the corner
chair.  Cousin Al leaves lettuce,
cherry tomatoes, cream cheese
chunks, bagel crumbs, and sesame
seeds scattered on the tablecloth
like a Sunday boater whose waves
uproot the reeds and slap the shoal.

It's not that I feel like I don't
belong here: my suit's just as clean
as everyone else's; my genealogy
and connection to the deceased
is as apparent as my nose.
It's just the air in the dining room
is as stiff as in that coffin,
and we all stand in line—
waiting—behind cousin Al—
waiting—with our paper plates
and plastic forks,
waiting our turn to dig holes
in Jell-O molds—waiting—
too apprehensive to cry out
or lift the lid.

**Brad Johnson**

## Our Gas Has Been Shut Off

Our gas has been shut off again, but this time
it's 38 degrees out and you can only ask so much

from a space heater.  Next week will be the water
and the phone but I'll write two bad checks

and hope to beat them to the bank by Friday.
If only I had the nerve to rob that bank or sleep with men

for money.  If only I could gain the courage
to steal a couple of antiques from Aunt June, sell them

on eBay.  As a waitress I should've taken money
from the till, overcharged customers and pocketed

the difference.  Maybe I could start selling cocaine
or create a meth lab in my basement.

                                    Outside the rain
pummels the rising riverbeds, forming ponds by the roadsides

and in the fields, giving temporary homes to ducks
whose white beaks disappear as they dive into the murky water.

And I'm on this couch, curled up in my favorite blanket,
two pair of socks on my feet, and on my third cup of hot tea,

re-reading a copy of *Wind in the Willows,* waiting for Mole
to come home and snuggle up by his fireplace.

**Amy Kitchell-Leighty**

## This Is Not My Stop

If a change is what you want,
we can tear up the floor.

Each night
while you sleep I can rearrange furniture,
put a couch in place of the TV
so we can watch each other until boredom.

If it's change, then we can wear wigs,
paint every other fingernail black and white,
get tattoos removed and your beauty mark.

You can spend the day without saying a word.

Newspaper the windows.
Chain the door handle.
Dig deep holes in the backyard
and fill them with salt water.

If you want a change, we can believe in miracles,
                                  shred up rose gardens,
perform deep betrayals,
                      and refuse forgiveness.

Or I could learn the piano,
write you sad love themes.
            I could break dishes
and wash each little piece.
                      You could dry.

We can go back to the beginning.  This time
you don't have to approach me.  I'll come
up to you.  I'll pay for everything
and be reckless at all the right moments.

We'll go back to
the beginning, thrift through
moments we want to keep.

When we take the boat out,
you can row, my hand feminine
cutting the water.

We'll give into firearms, the way they feel
and flash like heavy words.
We'll buy mace
and you can try it out on me.
We can stack everything
that has ever gone wrong between us
and name it one thing.

We can find a river
and name the river this word.

We can crunch it all together, feel it stark
on our skin,
never knowing the size of impossible.

If a change is what you want,
we won't have to.

      We'll change everything else.

**Jim Kober**

## Old Bean Hill Road

"Let's walk." It's midnight,
a mile and a half to our hotel.
"You're sure?" I ask.
"It's the country.
We've walked here before."

"What about the bridge?
No guard rails, you know.
If you fall in, I won't pull you out."
"The moon will reflect off
the old grey boards.
We'll be all right," he says.

Darkness except for
two parallel yellow curves.
He's in a tux.
I'm in heels.
Pebbles prick the soft leather.
"We'll be all right."
He's sure.

In a swamp frogs
croak next to tombstones
we saw that afternoon
askew in the cemetery
barely visible from the road
under orange yellow russet trees.
The heavy leaves clutch the night.

Halloween in Massachusetts.
Neighbors burned witches here.
Colonists and Indians were
hatcheted, shot,
bayoneted, raped,
pillaged, slaughtered,
left for dead here.
What corpses lie in
Old Bean Hill's fields?

A second cloud cloaks the moon.
"Walk in the rut," he says.
"It'll clear soon."
The bracken by the road
whisper about
psychopaths with knives,
Crazy Marys gone berserk,
the cold grasp of the unmourned hand.

Our footfalls on the bridge planks
give away our presence beneath
a mottled purple moon through greenish clouds.
"Ominous," he says.
Night presses on our skin
to keep strange fears in hand.
I speak of friends, our daughters,
the wedding dinner.
To hide his questions of the country night
he asks me to identify the sounds.

A car approaches—then another—
halogen lights.  They slow.
We stop and wait for the dark.
Free of the glare
the gravel road reflects
the moon above forbidding pines
in mist too thick for starlight.

We walk toward the light we know
through scarves of mist that curl around the trees
and breathe.

L. Leaf

## Sheltering Henry

Don't tell me not to do
what I need to do for Henry
who's been sleeping in a cemetery
for forty nights
even when rain pounds down
like small angry fists into the mud.
Henry is wet and cold.

Henry has a dent in his head
from a car crash in his youth,
the corner of his mouth sags down
when he says words starting with the letter "y."
Henry has trouble saying "yes."

The county welfare office also
has trouble saying yes
but for different reasons.
Henry's case worker has a supervisor
who speaks very slowly
and tells me Henry can't get shelter
because he caused his own dilemma.
She is wrong
and I can make her change her mind.
It's what I do.

I am a blizzard for two days
getting letters from doctors
dialing disconnected numbers
writing emails to the state.
I call the welfare director three times,
file for a hearing
shout and shake my fists without actually
doing either, the only way I know how
with regulations, threats of litigation.

Two days pass, and Henry sleeps among the graves
while I lie in my bed at night, warm
but without rest.
At the end of the third day
they give Henry shelter
in a boarding house.

The welfare director
complains to my colleague
that I am judgmental
and badgering.
Henry sleeps atop clean sheets,
the dent in his head
cradled in the cupped palm of his pillow.

**Michelle Lerner**

## Rowdy and Bleating

2 am, we'd put away
more than a few,
four of us crowded
into a small dented
blue Chevy, only two
whole legs between us,
McGuire hitting away
with his metal
crutch, our hair
messed up. We
were bleeding and
we'd run this red
light. Next there's
a siren and a cop
sticking his head in.
I think of belting
him with my new leg.
Instead I kind of
sink into my
coat, look sort of
shell-shocked, goofy,
and as he's about to
write out a summons,
I say, "Officer, I
don't know how, I mean
there's only two whole legs
between us all, sir."
And he flinches. It's as
if he's seen a kind
of freak. He twitches
and steps back with
"Oh my God," all flustered,
can't stumble back
fast enough, tells
us to take it slow
as we skid thru the
next light, fall
apart laughing, and
for a second there'd
never been Iraq.

**Lyn Lifshin**

68

## An Act of Kindness

She is one of the women
who travels daily from her township
Singing in the back of a pick-up truck
with a chorus of others
Come to clean the rooms
in my B & B bordering Kruger Park

She sees me walking a path
parallel to the Crocodile River
I see her running toward me
Watch her fall to her knees before me
Close the lowest five button holes
that fashion the front of my
ankle-length straight skirt

She says something in Swati
Looks up at me as a lilac-blue blossom
drops from a jacaranda tree
And under the kindness of shade
she pats my calves

I can't interpret the words
but I can read her body language
*There my dear*
*I've closed the open invitation*
*The accident that wrote itself*
*across your womanhood*
*I know this because here*
*no woman would walk*
*aware of bare thighs winking*
*between the weave of khaki*

I help her up
Hold her hardened hands
Thank her by returning
the sunshine of her smile
And waddle like a knobbellied duck
back to my room where I segregate
the unbefitting skirt to a suitcase

**Ellaraine Lockie**

## Bipolar

Five days deep into Alaska oceans
floating the eastern seaboard
in a city-block-sized boat
That bolsters four times the inhabitants
as my prairie hometown

I've quelled the queasiness
of motion sickness
Pardoned obnoxious bridge players
Cold-shouldered champagne shopping
And abstained from twenty-four hour
temptations of free-for-all food

Excepting the daily double doses
of Death by Chocolate Decadence
Whose just deserts demand
my walk on deck eight

Where passengers surpass
the saturation of a Singapore sidewalk
Shuffleboard discs slide between feet
And official photographers
enforce stops and fake smiles

My spasmodic steps synchronize
with squeeze breathing
from corset cruise compression
The wild animal in me captured and caged

One of three thousand passenger pets
confined to a bobbing zoo with railed bars
Claustrophobic even before I feel life's fragility
suspended in titanic augur
from overhung back-up boats

Followed by flash floods of foreboding
Cold sweat of fear washing me
to the side railing for support
A sardonic resolution
for halting breath and racing heart

Until a bald eagle
elevates me to 300-story heights
To the tops of blue white glaciers
Where tranquility is interrupted
only by calving clamor of ice
And where my fear is freeze dried

Then thawed fluid in frigid waters
Harborage for a humpback whale
breaching forty feet in front of me
His blowhole breathing never
hyperventilated by vacationing fish phobias

His vapor fountain frees compulsion
in my pressure cooker chest
And rhythmic repetition
of the ocean's respiration
is infectious in force
Pacemaker and pacific in effect
A prairie-like experience

**Ellaraine Lockie**

## Sitcom in a Café

We take her from The Facility
for a family drive and dinner

My ninety-one year old mother
Mostly deaf and nearly blind

Grabs paper cups of Catsup
partially-eaten hamburgers

and French fries from our plates
Says we paid for it all

As she deposits everything
into what she sees as her handbag

sitting on the floor
and slouching by her side

But we see it as my niece's
Guide Dog for the Blind in training

Gladly accepting the distinction
of the season's most fashionable fur purse

**Ellaraine Lockie**

## Graves

When my father turned to me, I didn't expect
to hear about their cemetery lots.  *"Hill top . . .
with a view."*   He spoke as if he described
prime real estate, the building lot a dreamer
buys for his bride while planning picture windows
and numbers of bathrooms and nurseries.

*"We won't be lonely."*  A litany
of neighbors, familiar names,
claimed nearby premium lots.
And for family, who wished
to join my father and mother,
extra sites were purchased.

*"Morning sun . . . and trees."*  In a voice
expectant and stirred by details
reflecting family luck and wisdom,
my father asked for my approval.

My grandfather's grave is in Brooklyn,
and I remember flowers planted by his stone.
One grandmother lies in Canton, and she never
saw her daughter's children.  I have
not seen her grave, but I have imagined
its small bulk and carved Chinese characters.

I remember eating roast pork buns
at the Brooklyn cemetery.  I watched
my father fill his bucket at a wall spigot
and water white lilies and peonies.

Grandmother and Mother walked
grassy cemetery rows reading aloud
Asian names and dates.  I ran my finger in
the cold crevices of tombstone words.
Grief held no body, no reality then.

But today, as I watch my father's
thin legs tremble, I know
his coffin, without windows,
cannot long remain empty.

A sparrow hovers and lands
on the porch railing as I begin
to speak about the beauty
of wind, sun, and hill top views.

**Florence McGinn**

## Payment

### I

As ice forms and thickens on juniper needles,
green branches against winter's bared sinews
sag and bend toward wind drifts of snow.

Debts are like that. The deepest debt forms,
soundless and transparent, around a raised spirit.
With time's passage and the weight of seasons,

a perceptible droop develops like a small grief.
As winds grip, a demand for payment
swirls and thickens around feet and legs.

The shadow lifts its face from stone and stretches
while I strain in brittle light to see if it is your form,
the translucent, folded shape you had before dying.

Do I make payment to remembered hands, centuries of bones,
the present moment forever quickening in the marrow of the past,
for the first breath, the never asked for flesh of life?

Do I acknowledge all I have been bequeathed from the whetted,
double edge of custom offered like a foothold, the first slippage
on a path resistant to claw marks scripted across granular ice?

If debt is genuine, I can never finish paying.

### II

The shadow grows in silence like an open
doorway, coalesces and rises against the silver
of my sight. I begin to believe I hear the dead

speak of ancestral sacrifices owed across generations
while practiced payments wither in my hands. My blood
account comes due with a cry like a young seal

cut from the herd by a white shark. Like the floundering
pup, I lift my head once, eyes wide, heart pounding
with understanding, and slip into sparkling flakes

of timelessness. Memory knows the spinning shape
struggling in airless, crimson waters, rising up
to define the surface it splinters and absorbs. I recognize

a familiar turn of head and know with icy certitude
that the only visible shadow is my own, its dark center,
an indentured substance pulsing with inherited flickers of light.

**Florence McGinn**

## Every Poem Is a Love Song to Death

The space between words, the deep
caesura separating the penumbra of small
letter *l* from the double ax of capital *T*, for instance,
is the blank cartridge that divides a heartbeat
and a heartbeat, a momentary incarnation
of the void, nesting place of all silence.

Eternity also sleeps in the distance
between voiced and unvoiced palatals, and between
the guttural hum of the *m* reclining and the forced march
of the *k*. You can almost see the letters shudder
with delight as one stutters to a close, exhausted,
to be answered across a universe of quiet
by the opening of the next—tiny flowers
of sound yielding to replacement that arrives
just in time to keep the garden blooming
another moment, then another.

                              We sing
to hold off the unassailable hush, but also
to become familiar with the grave-
light of the final period, the last
curl of the question mark that is a ringlet,
or perhaps a scar, on the forehead of God,
with the silence that stretches from this chair
where I decipher my own scrawl
to nowhere.

**Michael McIrvin**

## The Place I Dream of When I Dream of Home

Here is the house on the corner, white with green shutters.
These are the five steps I climbed thousands of days,
never once imagining there would be a last time.
Here are the purple, lavender, and white lilacs
growing along the shed. The combination to that lock is 6-20-26.
This is the rock garden where my mother planted tulips.
Here is where I grew a skin that wouldn't be shed for years.
Across the street is the park and the pond where you
skip stones, ripples expanding into concentric circles,
where ducks congregate, quacking for breadcrumbs.
That's the rock fireplace ice skaters huddle around in winter.
There. That hill is called Suicide, where the girl in
the plaid skirt and her brother in the salt-and-pepper pants
gave me a bloody nose and pushed my sled down to the bottom.
Here is the tree I read in, nestled between branches.
I watched people from that perch in the sky. This stone bridge
was 'safe' in bike tag. Here is the softball diamond where
mornings I pitched for the pee-wee team and afternoons
played second base for the juniors. And this.
This is the greenhouse. I came here to be alone.
Here is the fountain filled with coins by those wishing for something else.
That sound? That's the ice cream truck two streets over,
playing an old tune, gathering the children in.

**Terry Martin**

## Around the Corner of Midnight

He's gonna' drink that ale
and watch the action,
see what there is to see,
catch a dance or two if somethin'

long-legged 'n lovely catches his eye.
He's gonna' dance real close,
slink tight to her swivel 'n
just about die wanting to look

to see do I notice.
Then he'll sit with his boys,
his fingers pushing circles of wet
glass-sweat across the tiny table top,

while he scans the room,
so he won't appear to be
in a hurry to strut over here.
Yeah, I see him over there,

hangin' out 'n lookin' cool
in tight jeans 'n gold chains,
but if he wants me, he's gonna'
have to show me just what it is he's got.

I ain't walkin' around the corner
of midnight for just any guy.
I only got one heart 'n right now
it still belongs to me.

**Lorraine Merrin**

**La Loba**
(A Native-American Legend)

an old woman surviving
on thunder and lightening

travels plains and prairies
gathering bones

bones bleached by the sun
bones blessed by the moon

but only one type
the bones of the wolf

a hip bone, a rib cage, a skull
collected and treasured until

there is enough
to make an entire skeleton

this bone sculpture
is a cradle of incubation,

the old woman sings her song
la loba - la loba

a hip bone, a rib cage, a skull,
flesh out - become furred

the creature comes into being,
its tail curls, it breathes,

opens its eyes and leaps away
running towards the horizon

the old woman smiles – the wolf
shifts in the moonlight

a maiden fades into the night

**Les Merton**

## Ravaged Roses

When my roses bloom, Japanese
beetles zoom in like kamikazes,
gobble great holes
until a mound of hard brown scarabs
too gorged to fly
hangs from the sepals
where a flower used to be.

I struggle to contain my rage, curb
the impulse to crack each carapace
between my fingers or crush
them one by one under my heel
until digested particles of ruined rose
ooze from their broken bodies.

I am a reasonable person,
willing to negotiate.  I disapprove
of traps and poisons.  I respect
their right to live, would share
my roses if they would agree
to leave each second rose,
or even every third, for me,
or if they would forbear
from gluttony at least
until the flowers start to fade.

I want to teach them principles
of sustainable consumption,
persuade them that restraint
will help the bush survive to feed
them for another season. Yet,
heedless of all reason, they keep
ravaging my roses while I remain

at war with myself, as helpless
before this huge hunger
as any impotent god
watching the world's splendor
swallowed by greed.

**Joyce Meyers**

## The Body Reflects on the Future

> On being diagnosed with
> breast cancer at 51

One day the Body will look in the mirror
and see her image slowly turn black,
her face erased
as if smeared by God's thumb,
a sign on her chest in letters of blood:
"FOR RENT – Historic property, built 1952.
Previous owner a little old lady.
Many rooms never used."

One day the Body will look in the mirror
and see a woman who is
no longer there,
swaddled like a mummy in crime-scene tape,
encircled by a trio of lamprey-mouthed crones
with scissors instead of hands.

One day the Body will look in the mirror
and see a woman who is not herself,
a woman made of nothing
but clacking bones,
outré in a Schiaparelli gown of cobwebs
and a wig of platinum-blonde worms.

Today the Body looks in her mirror
and glimpses a woman she has not yet met,
her neck festooned with a garland of breasts
plucked from women who no longer need them,
a woman who launders rotting nightgowns
in a bathtub filled with blood,
who beckons with gestures vague as mist
but fingers sharp as scythes,
a woman who is still half a world away
but whose dark van is cruising toward the airport.

**Pamela Miller**

**The Surrealist Body**

*With apologies to André Breton*

My body with its hair of wild rice and ice storms
Its hair that unfurls from a pirate's mast
Its thoughts encased in amber that breathes like a membrane
topped off with a fez of forgetfulness
My body with its waist of secret code
Its laughingstock waist, an hourglass gone haywire
where time sifts dizzily backwards
My body with its mouth full of men's names chewed to ribbons
My body with a tongue of plague and cholera
With its tongue a locked suitcase
With teeth infiltrated by elderly Japanese spies
My body with temples of sparks and götterdämmerung
With a brain where my Muse loafs defiantly in her bathrobe
My body with shoulders of avalanches and wingbuds
My body with fingers of stuttering lightning
With fingers like bridges to nowhere
With arms of wild regattas and crumbling caryatids
My body with legs of thunderous diminuendos
moving like Laurel and Hardy with tarantulas in their trousers
My body with feet of ugly stepsisters and bunioned glass slippers
With tortoise-shell feet, with feet of broken English
My body with its morose left breast full of sour milk and curdled blood
My body with its Frankenstein breasts caressed by surgeons' knives
Its breasts of subterranean secrets and unknown rendezvous
My body with its belly like a brioche that feeds multitudes
Its belly of neon and cymbals
My body with its back of Roman ruins
With its back a down escalator to the earth's chaotic core
With its letter-bomb back
My body with its hips of tomahawks
Its boxing-ring hips where the palooka's trunks catch fire
My body with its buttocks of Alaskan waterfalls
My body with its buttocks of cruel and unusual punishment
My body with its potentate buttocks
My body with its sex of paper
My body with its sex turned inside out
My body with its recluse sex, peeking out from behind her veils
My body with its eyes like opals in mayonnaise
Its eyes of bat caves and collapsing stars
My body with its eyes still too nearsighted to see
the next world being built beyond my bones

Pamela Miller

## Address Book

Last night, cleaning out the desk,
I found an old address book
bent and battered, pages yellowed, curled,

the cover a mottled blue,
stained with ink, wine, coffee,
who knows what else?

It had been there in the corner of a drawer
for years now.  I opened it with care
half-imagining that small, exotic birds

would fly out of it, chirp for a moment,
and fall dead at my feet.
I fixed on a name: "Biancamaria Tedeschini-Lalli,"

and suddenly Italy, 1972, seemed present in the room:
faces of students, scenes in streets, the decor of pensiones,
the clock tower in Venice, my son Stephen, then 4, in awe of it,

an Italian friend, Osvaldo Croce,
piggy-backing my son Nick across the Piazza San Marcos,
the nostalgia so thick now I can't see the present.

I turn the page to "Lee Saitta,"
my sister, an X through the name,
dead—how many years now?—in Salt Lake,

and "Ben Santoli," my old sidekick,
dealing cards in Vegas for decades,
out of touch with him since the '70s.

I can't flip through much more of this.
Closing the book, I think about throwing it away,
but put it back instead in the corner

of the drawer where it came from, carefully,
like a rabbi returning the torah to its sacred place.
A scripture reminding me who I am.

**Fred Moramarco**

## Menopause Dream

It comes every quarter like late
menstruation,  a belated full
moon, a hollowness buried
in the gut.  I see a pod

cocooned in flesh and blood,
layers peeling in time-lapse speed;
then a maroon vein bursts.  Still birth
and blackness.

Only the heart flutters, skips
a beat, then drops hollow
point bullets in my
stomach.  Uterus mortis,

eggs shrivel into raisins baked
in the oven of half a century.
Grief spreads like nightshade;
its purple-veined bellies

choke the brilliance
from the burning brush.
This type of loss felt only
once before at my sister's death.

Awake at three a.m.,
a single candle flame eclipses
the rim of my wine glass
just like the summer

sun halos on my daughter's
blonde hair. Why is one
child enough for thirty
years, and then is not?

**Carmel L. Morse**

## Phone Call

I can see the River Jordan
from where I am sitting.
Not really a river, more like a ditch.

This morning I had a meeting
with a teacher whose daughter
died in a car crash nine years ago.
Then she lost her son in the army.

I am involved in a research project,
I work hard on projects, projects,
and lose my temper with some students.

My students sit at their brown desks
and dream of colours and Purim and sex
and the weather is getting warmer.

This time last month
we were in bed together.

Sounds like a boring grammar lesson:
She lost her children.
I lose my temper.
They are losing their concentration.

I don't ever want to lose you.

**Nora Nadjarian**

**After You**

I do the minimum to keep up
my end of housekeeping—
pay the bills, dry the dishes, and take out the trash
while you do the real work.  If I were alone
this house would soon regress.
Cobwebs would trail across the gritty floors,
the dogs would snooze on the couch,
the vacuum cleaner would no longer inhale
and the garden would dry up
though other plants would take over.
But I'd make do driving to Safeway for toilet paper,
kibble and frozen pizza.

It would be a new life, another regression of sorts:
me and the dogs and my thoughts of you.
I'd sit on the porch watching the light leave the sky
and when the owls began to hoot
and your face had dissolved into darkness
I'd go inside to seek you among the photographs,
the music in the piano bench,
and the tarnished candle sticks
that once held trembling flames.

I'd gradually withdraw from the future.
There'd be nothing to look forward to—
the smell of rice pilaf and garlic,
watching videos side by side,
your breathing when I wake up.
Immersed in the eternal presence
of clouds and morning stiffness,
the ridge of a dog's back,
I'd slip into the world
that was always there
before you.

**Peter Nash**

## My Work

I keep track of the comings and goings of people.
My work is very simple.  I write down and retain
the information that others give me.

When I started here they came in every day
with two lists of names to alphabetize.
First I added the names of those who had just come.
Then I crossed out the names of those who were gone.

Now the task is easier, but not as challenging.
We have instituted a number system.  Numbers
are faster to find and take less space in the books.

I didn't agree with the change to numbers because
I thought they would be easy to transpose.  But now
I realize that the volume of people coming and going
makes this change to numbers essential.

I tell myself, "I go home every night to my family.
My job isn't my whole life.  If accuracy
doesn't matter to them, why should it to me?"

I'm proud I don't bring my work home with me.
The only time I think about work there is when
I see and smell the smoke coming from
the tall smokestacks on the other side of town.
                           —Poland, 1944

**Ann Floreen Niedringhaus**

86

## Early

I watch for you and breathe in
thick winter fog, breathe out
steamy aromatic memories
I had inhaled when last with you.
I balance the breaths, juggle
the frosty earth and whitened plants,
the pale smudge in the sky that is the sun,
the paler smear that is the moon,
the icy malingering mud,
the dark matter between celestial bodies,
all on the one hand, while on the other,
your earlobe held by my lips, your
suddenly hot cheek, your tropical sigh.
I stare at the horizon, my eyes fixed for you,
and I am already with you, I am open.
Starlings and juncos mistake the fog
frozen on my eyes for infinite sky.
Turning, wheeling, squawking
squadrons of black birds enter my open eyes
and fill my entire body with their wild cries.
They exult and sing and their flapping wings
tickle and heat me as I stand waiting,
watching for you to arrive
with your beauty and sweet hot breath.

**Leonard Orr**

## Security

Homeland security can be grasped by
assuming a defensive posture, dropping
in unison and lying on our left sides, my legs
bent under and against your legs, your
right hand reaching around my right hip,
my right arm wrapped around your ribs
right and then left and comforting every
soft smoothness; then the homeland will be
secure for the present. The covers should
be up to our necks, for warmth and privacy,
and there should be enough light so that
I can see the color of your hair just
before my eyes. Once we are secure enough
that way, we shift by an agreed upon signal,
to avoid panic and maintain such well-being,
encoded and decoded and transmitted
through our central nervous systems,
onto our right sides and repeat. As we feel
the security alert change, we turn again
so I am on my back and you are above me
and we whisper the night's secrets, keeping
lips to ears, or breathing in Morse code.
If we fear surveillance, we slide undercover.
Whenever we are out, thanks to these pamphlets,
we can search each other *sub rosa*, quietly
pat each other down, infiltrate, assess and deploy.
We surge against insurgency, check every
thread and layer, every button, every zipper,
every earring, every fold, every hidden place,
safer and calmer, better and better.

**Leonard Orr**

## Yiddish for Travelers

I bought the book optimistically,
thinking to go there one day, to that lost land
where the border guards only know Yiddish,
where you hold out your passport and say,
"Awt iz mein pas. Tsee muz ich alts ayfennen?"
Must I open everything? And they let you pass,
you are okay with them. At the Post Office
you buy stamps engraved with fuzzy portraits
of Jacob Glatstein and Itzik Manger,
postcards of Mani Leib and Boris Tomashevsky.
The villages are all picturesque shtetls; you can
arrange for a tour by carriage and pass some nights
in centuries-old, thick-timbered shuls.
People gather to watch flickering black and white films
like *Green Fields* and *Die Meshugener*, and to
kvell whenever the lists of Nobel Prize winners
are published, to analyze the names and hab naches from the Jews.
Stay a long time; you can always go to a Yiddish bank and change
your dollars into the Yiddish money, or you say,
"Ich hab reisencheckn," and they take the traveler's check.
In the capitol of the Yiddish country, there are
shiny green, blue, and yellow trolleys, broad plazas
with delis and patisseries, where the small tables
are filled with people reading and arguing and joking
over their strudel and rugelach, sipping tea in glasses.
They place sugar cubes in their mouths; they love herring.
They squeeze plump cheeks of nephews and grandchildren.
The people there are all oddly reminiscent of my relatives,
my aunts and uncles and great aunts and great uncles,
and all of their relatives who I never met, who never
somehow crossed over, who were isolated perhaps
into this landlocked Yiddish land where the police
speak Yiddish, where everyone is in terrific health,
vigorous and sometimes portly from all the pastries,
from the lack of stress, from having escaped
everything so thoroughly.

**Leonard Orr**

## Yoga Practice

I keep trying to practice yoga,
but I can't follow the directions.
I can't send my spine skyward
or sink my sitting bones into the earth.
Only you could make me extend
such distances, rise and sink
simultaneously, and only you
know just where my sitting bones are.
I am so distracted by the lovely words,
*Adho Mukha Svanasana, Dandasana,*
and I chew the syllables, tossing them
in my mouth left to right like jujubes,
*danda danda dandasana,* and I fail
to check that my pelvic rim is parallel to the floor
(I need your hands to find my pelvic rim, to see
my thighbones are grounded, *feefifofum,*
*ramalamadandasana*), that my spine is lengthened.
I can't even breathe properly; each inhale,
each exhale, a word like exile, should be all.
I am instructed to count, to think
*only inhale, only exhale,* but my thoughts
sink and rise and search you out
(what do you look like when you do this?),
or *sitting forward bend* (my, but you bend
so beautifully I want to wrap myself
around you and bend with you, inhale
with you, exhale with you, like so).
*Paschimottanasana,* feeling the heat of you
really helps me concentrate, my back
rolls and melts and can flow both
skyward and earthward, my pelvic rim
is clear to me now, syllables sweet
and sticky, my lying-draped-around-you bones
are in especially good order and my breath
seeps uncounted and audible exactly
in rhythm with yours.

**Leonard Orr**

Remembrance

I remember the color of your eyes
but not their shade.

I remember your feminine shape,
but the terrain of your body
has all but eroded from my memory.

Time is a thief.
He has silently crept through the shadows of my mind,
stealing you from me piece by piece.
Your fragrance, your voice, your laugh –
all plunder in Time's larceny.

But your lips . . . .

At night when I stand in the chilled desert breeze
and feel it lightly kiss my face,
I close my eyes and feel the phantom of your lips against mine

and remember.

David Parke

## Dollmaking

The doll we have decided to make
is called Popette. Cut from the pattern
of all the other Popettes.

Take for your rib a slip of French Bisque
to pour into her mold like heavy cream.
She should pour steadily.

Breathe air in through a small hose
to clear holes and prevent blockages.
Leave her to set.

Break mold apart gently
so as not to shatter the tender form.
Soak her in sixties reruns
to soften for sculpting.

Scrape seams to Barbie curves.
Cut out child-like eye openings
with your feather knife. Trim fingers
to fit around mascara wands
and stiff cocks. Shape toes
to run for another twist-top.

Close your eyes and rub
fingers over her parts
to make sure she's flawless.
Rinse her in clear water
ready for vitrification.

Laid on a bed of sand,
purified and hardened
in the fires of Easy Bake ovens,
roasted in locker-room jokes,
her soft green clay transforms
to bright, brittle porcelain.

Attach the cloth body with glue
and tight wax cords.
Fill her opening with soft white seed
and stitch her up.

Dress her in the style of your choice –
little black dress, or white ruffled apron.
She'll wear whatever pleases you.

**Rae Pater**

**Poem for My Daughter to Read
Ten Years Hence**

Half naked on the couch,
screams muffled
in a crumpled afghan,
you ball up on knees and elbows,
derriere where your face would be
if you were sitting:  this
because you cannot find your leotards.

To make it better for us all
I clown a quick story
about leotards leaping free
in the front yard,
shaping themselves with snow.

Listening now,
you unfold red-eyed
as they come dancing in,
melting blue on the carpet
where they crawl slowly under the couch,
one toe barely showing, crimped
like a knit brow.

Still determinedly grim,
you reach down without a word,
bring them up and quickly slide
your legs as deep as they will go.

Ten years hence, fifteen and smiling,
perhaps you'll shake your head at this:
"No, Dad, not me . . ." to which
I'll say, "Oh yes . . ." and then,
with a more convincing voice, quote
your grandfather:  "More truth than poetry."

**Roger Pfingston**

## The Kiss

You've gone off to work
    but your blotted lips
O up at me

from the wastebasket
    where I've just tossed
a Kleenex of my own,

neither brightly marked
    nor spread
with such syllabic fun,

mine balled up, a purge
    of consonants
beside your lovely vowel.

**Roger Pfingston**

## Missing Man, September 11, 2006

After the Pinot Grigio,
    the mandarin chicken
and stir-fry peas,
    the three of us
drink in
    the Rose of Sharon scent
on the breeze
    through the kitchen window.
Even
    with your chair empty,
we resist
    the tug
of memory:
    the towers falling
in a lust
    of evil's gravity.

The three of us sit—
    husband, wife, widow—
in a wine-blessed buzz.
    The late summer night
is sweet enough
    to half-convince us
that the world
    is a lush
and companionable
    place,
and that you
    have just
left the room
    to grab a bottle
of Merlot.

**Ronald  Pies**

## Apple Spider

My niece at age four
is already tired
of the language as we
know it.  Instead
of orange juice she asked
for a glass of apple
spider and at lunch
at a diner in town
she wanted me to put
a quarter in the little
juice box next
to the table and play
a song.

When we got home
I walked up into her
bedroom in search
of some sort of proof
that she is what I always
suspected: a genius.
Perhaps there would be
books on linguistics,
philosophy, Shakespeare
or essays by Pound
who might have ignited
her passion to "make it new."

But there was nothing
by Plato under her purple
hippo, no critical works
amongst her coloring
books or Socrates hidden
behind her dolls.  Later
when her mother claimed
her daughter can't even
read and the classics
for a four-year-old
are Barney and Lamb Chop,
I still wasn't convinced.

So when my niece
told me she heard
I liked poet trees,
then asked where do
they grow, we both
picked up our cold
glasses of root beard,
held on to each other's
hand, then headed out

the door to see if any
were growing in
the backyard.

**Kevin Pilkington**

## Parthenon

When you arrived in Athens
you discovered the Acropolis
was never named after a diner
down on Second Avenue and
the Parthenon could never fit in
your hand the way it always did
with coffee to go in a paper cup.
Your hotel was just blocks away.
At night you sat on the roof staring
at the ancient ruin, lights shining
on it—lit up like an old man
on good wine.

The next day you toured the Acropolis,
so amazed you kept taking photos
of the Berilie gates, a few
columns, next the east cella, another
of a blonde in tight shorts. You pick
up a stone to put in your pocket
as a souvenir and to weigh you
down against the wind that kept
knocking your cap off like a bully
from the grammar school near Plaka.
Below the east pediment stronger
gusts blow dust off the ground,
spinning it into a statue of Athena
who stares into your face until
another gust blows her away.

In the Acropolis museum
a young statue of a sixth century
boy holds onto a calf that is
draped over his shoulders like
a sweater. You admire him since
you were never able to hold onto
anything for that long in your life.
Near him is a maiden with the kind
of curves in her stone you couldn't help
noticing. Even with her hands missing
along with a bit of nose, she still
looks hot and hasn't put on an ounce
of marble around the hips for centuries.

Outside you stop to look down at Athens,
that in the distance under the bright sun
looks like a path made of white pebbles,
and beyond it the sea. You decide
to go for a swim and now
that you are convinced it takes more
than one god to run a universe,

you are able to jump up on a wall,
step down on rooftops and stroll
all the way to the Aegean.

Kevin Pilkington

**Coloring Death**

Orange was the shade of base
on my grandmother's brow.
Crimson: the rouge on her cheeks.
Black: everyone's shirt.
Blue: the sky that day.

Yellow was the colored paper
Mrs. Loots, my dear seventh-grade teacher,
printed sonnets on
when I returned to class that afternoon
with pink cheeks.
My tears were clear. The sky
was blue. Grandma's blouse
was floral and vibrant.
The ink of the program was black, the smudge
on my fingertips,
when she was buried, was black,
and later that afternoon,
when I clutched those sonnets,
trying to understand, my fingertips
were black again. The music
was generic,
the grass was green,
and her mascara was black.

Brown was the casket
my father hoisted outside.
His muscles quivered in thirty-second notes
as he walked into the blue sky,
onto the green grass.
We followed, and we didn't question
the bright sunlight, didn't think
that it should be any cloudier.
Instead, we squinted
until rainbow rays spread
across our vision, understanding only
that it hurt our tear-heavy eyes to look.

**Lucas Pingel**

## Maria Dances and All I Can Do Is Drink

She stands in front
of the big band, her hands
not rigid blades, but a relaxed
mist of the wave,

scanning the rocky coastline—
a hang glider plumed over
the foamy coast.  Her hips
rock gently, the music
dissolving into her veins like wine.

I sip my whiskey, sharp
and bitter, my head tilts
like a trumpet flare upstage.

I want to be lost,
to feel that magical sway of her
champagne ponytail.  Her sand
freckled neck.  Her
warm jellyfish legs

that keep moving to sculpt
this basin of sound, growing
and shrinking, growing
and shrinking, billowing
in and out
like the lungs of the sea.

Lucas Pingel

## Bombazine
*n. a worsted silk dyed black for mourning wear*

A thirdhand acquaintance with death,
Japan black trunk with brass hasp

opened, rank with stale sweat and trace of violet eau de cologne
still, Suzie's gloat to have for dress-up
       her late grandmother's trappings,

swathes of jet-dark fabric, (dresses, countless buttons),
       a dingy fox tippet
we array, and the material puddling around us like pillow lava.

Calling ourselves Mrs. Uppity and Mrs. Whosit,
       we traipse the attic.
Suzie's terrier mix watches, blinking from an oblong of sunlight.

A pair of houseflies harry, circling the naked ceiling bulb,
jumble of hat boxes and empty picture frames
       tottery at our tread.

With the deliciousness of being all grown-up,
       we peer through make-believe lorgnette,
a fraction of time like a soot curlicue from the
       snuffed candle,

not a thought that our "bombazine" regalia represents
       twenty-five years of widowhood.

Patricia Polak

## Caravan-ing

Aromatics of a Middle Eastern port city:
        diesel fuel and tamarisk
        brine of the Mediterranean meets
            parching desert sirocco
        brazier coals and sewerage
        teasing linger of pungent, jewelescent
            spice bazaar.

Square with cadres of men in sun-glared white shirts.

A guttural hawked chant:
        *Homs-Hama, Homs-Hama* from long-distance drivers,
        and counterpoint other driver-touts
        pharyngeal *Haleb-Haleb-Haleb*
        (for the place conversant Westerners know as
            Aleppo, Syria).

Wraithlike burka-robed women thread the heat-baked square.

Accompanying small children stride with dirty toes in their
        leather sandals—seemingly free as colts.

We must hard-bargain (scrawling on a pad pounds and piastres;
        dickering on the blazing taxi's hood) to go from here,
        Latakia, to Aleppo.

*This* the Valhalla of the vintage Mercedes-Benz—flying
        the roads and, moreover, tanking it across the desert,
        where the endless shifting dunes yield to hard-packed
        tracks.

Our Mercedes once cream-colored—now weather-bleached,
        opalescent, and useless to inquire mileage because the
        shanty-housed car mechanics never let them die.

Amplified, reverberant, the muezzin, suppliant to Allah,
        cries out our departure time.

The Syrian has sold every possible place for the ride . . .
        and then some.

The car will barrel at top speed, all but the driver's
        door half ajar.

Jam of genial, swarthy Middle Easterners nearly fallen
        out of the speeding Mercedes, clutching the open
        window frames as the desert-cooked slipstream wallops.

Celadon-green worry beads dangle, swaying from the rearview
        mirror, making a chittery click-clack.

Roly-poly, pistachio-munching driver tunes the radio to an
   ear-piercing ululation and tambourine-heavy music
   until a sliver of crescent-topped minaret augers Aleppo,
   ancient and historic.

The Mercedes' engine ticks down.  Completed caravan.

**Patricia Polak**

## Urban Homesteading

a jab of chemical,
> the handyman Brassos the entrance railing

bricks in rusty-red registers
> punch-holed with reflective window ports

the polar masquerade of air conditioners
> in flush-set oblongs

step down into a checkerboard of lobby
> with dusty savannah of planter ferns

once Conestogas drawn by yoked oxen
> cut a pioneering swath of track

across plains—
> the loam so fertile-rich and depthless

now, a pre-war Otis (numerously mechanic-ed),
> hoists upward a dozen floors

urbanite paranoia of locks
> keyed open to the welcoming familiar

a cubby of an apartment's refuge
> from a native's love-hate relationship

with strumpet-goddess Manhattan,
> her extremes of wealth and want

her million price-tagged opiates
> against life's capricious transience

Patricia Polak

## By the Window

I used to put your baby chair in front of the big pane-glass window
facing the backyard.

You were tranquil and quiet as I watched your spirit lift,
soon lost inside the dance of leaves of the tall tree outside.

At five months, you would stare for what seemed hours,
cooing at the melodic motion of leaves, your hands and feet moving,
synchronized with each turn of the tree's kaleidoscope of light.

As the afternoon would drip down upon me,
I found tasks to do, not far away, and I would listen . . .
imbibe your gentle baby sounds, feeling certain that you would grow to love nature,
knowing that I must be doing something right to have such a calm baby.

I didn't know then
that the temporary disappearance from this world
was only the beginning of autism.

It was the dawning of other worlds
of prisms that would take you from us,
that would take language from you.

It was genesis of a specific kind of spinning
that would yearn to make the picture whole, centered,
to make the light and its refraction seem just right.

It is a time encapsulated in my mind
when I could not have known where your silent motion would take us.
Yet I still cannot separate from it, still cannot disengage from that time
when I knew where certainty ended and began.

Yet, you walk in the living room today,
a young man with straight brown hair,
taller than I, slender and carrying a blanket you've had since you were three.

You go to the couch by the window, cover yourself in warmth,
place your head on the distinct edge of the couch pillow,
and watch the leaves dance above you on the trellis outside,
adjusting your position to merge with all I cannot comprehend.

You smile in a satin and oceanic serenity I have rarely seen in another,
become immersed in the incandescence of the entirety of this one day,
this one afternoon from which I cannot disengage,
and I realize that you have grown
and have grown to love nature,

and, as much as I have lost and found you
in all the waltzes of leaves and light,
that I must have done something right.

**Connie Post**

I catch the droplet in midair on its way to my lap.

Clear as glycerin, it is suspended briefly as I dig for a tissue,
       twisting in my plastic seat on the Broad Street subway
on this raw day that makes mucus drip and steam rise from the vents.
I am among my own kind.
                Invisible in plain sight
we occupy our bodies. We make ourselves at home.

      By the door a chubby twelve-year-old slouches
against her brother and sucks her thumb.
              A college student
hugs a backpack to his chest, gnawing his thumbnail in pursuit
of an unattainable scrap at the very quick. ·

      My eyes droop in the overheated car
like the toddler's across the aisle.  In down jacket
and tiny Timberlands he dozes as a trail of snot advances
       toward his upper lip.  His mother swipes at it
       with the corner of his blanket.

Once on this train at midday I watched a man in work clothes
eat green beans from an open can, tossing back
his head with each shake of the tin.

      On the 34 trolley, second leg of my journey,
two teenagers huddle.  The air between them
                  breathes
with each slow movement of their hands as they feed each other
       Slim Jims leathery with salt, cheese puffs
       sheening his fingers in day-glo orange,
           and for dessert, a glutinous pink cake
        like an overturned teacup, halved by her nail
        and offered to his lips.

      When their meal is over and the wrappers
crushed tenderly underfoot,
       they lean toward each other
           in a soft and sticky kiss.

      I can taste it from eight rows back.

Julie Preis

## Jukebox Dancing

We drive past Macdona, Dunlay, Hondo,
D'Hanis. And what pours out of us is
uncertainty. Is this truly us? Then two miles
shy of Sabinal, a Highway Patrol cruiser pulls
even and for one single moment hesitates—I
think of black-chinned hummingbirds poised
before the nectar—and we blossom with exhilarating
fear. The interior of this Buick Riviera is made
of red leather and feels as sensual as courtship.
There is a tennis racket on the floor, an infant's
pacifier in the glove box. We are possessed.
It has been a suffocating summer, but now we
listen for an eerie lightness in our laughter—like
the underside of some terrible affliction. At
Knippa we cross the Frio River and soon afterwards
turn north. There is a strange falling away with
each new mile. At Garner Park we climb
exhausted into the evening heat. There is physical
loneliness in each new step, an indulgent pleasure
that cannot tell itself from loss. We leave the
keys in the ignition. Three years ago, when I was
twelve, I rode here with my parents. We hiked
past canyons, mesas, limestone cliffs. I vanished
far inside myself and wouldn't come out. But now
we stand beside this bigtooth maple and marvel
at Rio Grande turkeys, black rock squirrels,
hayhurt's scallopwing skippers. We are warm and
swollen from our impulsiveness. We do not ask how
we'll get home. We are abandoned in a way that feels
both bottomless and hopeful. We wait for dusk—
when the jukebox music will begin in the concession
building. We tell ourselves that every skein of emotion
will finally braid together. The night will grip us with
impersonal tenderness—and every tremor of unease
will float away. Unbounded feeling will rise up, and I
will pull you in my arms, your face a moonlit oval.
And we will dance.

**Doug Ramspeck**

## River Woman

What he feels is as deafening as chorus
frogs in breeding season, like something
hiding behind the jaundiced moon
above his barn. When he spies her
by the river he imagines that the heavy
current will capture him and carry him
downstream until he drowns.

On Sunday morning he watches her suckling
her infant child on the back porch,
watches her hanging her clothes on the line.
He has never said a word to her,
she has never said a word to him—but longing
creeps into his ears like burrowing earwigs,
swarms like pomace flies on rotting fruit.

He makes a potion of snakeroot,
thimbleweed, corn cockles, celadines,
lupines, skullcaps, and everlastings—
then drinks until the cup is dry.
But that afternoon while working in the fields
he envisions her scooping from beneath
her blouse that pale white breast—

hypnotic as the water moccasin's mouth
before it strikes—and that night
he dreams that he is standing at her window
and looking in to where she's sleeping
by her husband. The infant child hisses
like a snake inside the crib. He tries to speak
but air escapes from fang wounds in his throat.

In the morning he finds a dead pileated
woodpecker on his dock beside the river,
and at dusk he hears her singing from her porch—
her voice as plaintive as the hoot owl—
so he gathers from the woods destroying angels,
Caesar's mushrooms, jack-o'-lanterns—
and vows to swallow them for supper.

**Doug Ramspeck**

## Strip Mall Apocalypse

Inland the ash suspends itself above the city as plainsong.
Where once were strip malls
                            above the thrown-back head
of ocean cliffs, where once was the Wal-Mart
            and the Taco Bell and the Radio Shack,
now there is the nursery of flame and the acrid shadow
                                    and the malignant
emptiness of sidewalks and parking lots
and high-rises.
                        Here is where the darkened birds
impale themselves in sand, where the great embroidery
of dead fish bob as preternatural stench in the shallows,
when the sun is an embryonic scab in a blank sky.
                                    It is Odysseus
who has commandeered the rowboat,
who wears his Abercrombie T and aims the bow
into the rising arc of waves.
                        If once he hitched the ox and donkey
to the plow, if once he sowed his fields with salt
and played at madness, now he leans his weight into the oars
and watches the city of Polyphemus
                                pluck out its last eye.
And though once he heard the cry of the betrayed men
devoured by Scylla leaking darkly from his ears
                                    as prodigal blood,
now he listens through his earphones to the last scratchings
            from an iPod, and all he carries with him
to the sea is a little irony and duct tape.  Argos has long since
given up and died.  No one shoots the arrow through
                                the twelve axe heads.
Even the sirens are exhausted from the bump and grind.
And if all his life he's been waiting for someone to ask him
                        why he carries the winnowing fan,
today there's only rowing to be done.  And ash to swallow.
And the dulled raiment of eyeless days and nights above the cliffs.

Doug Ramspeck

## The Possessed

Long before the arrests, the suicides of Nikolai
and Kirillov, the murder of Shatov, the death
of his own father and Marya, Peter played baseball
on a Little League team near Cincinnati. The name
of the team was "The Tipton Forks Devils," and he played
second-string third base, though in truth his mind
often wandered beneath the heavy Ohio sun.  Sometimes
as he sat on the bench he wondered about the Great Order
of Things, but mostly he imagined a ball flying off a bat
then soaring up to seek infinity, or he would
grow weary of seeing his father plopped soberly in the stands.
During those rare moments when Peter actually played,
his father would chide him for fielding ground balls
as casually as though gathering strange stones along a beach,
for running the bases as though he believed it were a stroll.
His father was all about subservience, of course,
about sacrificing yourself for the greater team and the final
score; but Peter always figured it was just a game,
and not a very interesting one at that.  Sometimes he imagined
God hiding in the webbing of his glove, but mostly he figured
he was all alone, that nothing in his life would ever matter,
which is probably why he astonished everyone one Saturday
by fielding a ball, pivoting with a sudden and surprising intensity,
and flinging it into the stands toward his father's head.

**Doug Ramspeck**

**Birch Street**

Sitting on the porch outside my walk-up with Elaine,
watching the Friday-night action on Birch Street.
Southside's so humid the air weeps.

Me and Elaine are weeping too.
Silent tears of solidarity.
She's so full of prozac she can't sleep and
I'm so drunk I can't think straight.
Her depression and my beer free our tears
from the jail we carry in our hearts.

Neighbors and strangers pass by in the water vapor.
Walking in twos and fours.  Driving by in souped-up
cars and wrecks.  Skinny, greased-up gangbangers
with pants so big they sweep the street and girl friends
in dresses so tight they burn my eyes.

I can smell Miguel's Taco Stand.  Hear the cool
Mexican music he plays.  Sometimes I wish Elaine
were Mexican.  Hot, sweet and the ruler of my passion,
but she's from North Dakota, a silent state where
you drink to feel and dance and cry.

Sailing, drifting down Birch Street.  Misty boats,
street shufflers and señioritas.  Off to their somewhere.
I contemplate how empty my can of beer is and
how long can I live with a woman who cries all day.

Mondays are better.  I sober up and lay lines for the
Gas Company.  Good clean work. Work that gives me
time to think about moving to that little town in central
Mexico I visited twenty years ago before Birch Street,
Elaine and three kids nailed my ass to this porch.

**Charles P. Ries**

**Los Huesos**
*(the bones)*

I sit with the dead tonight.  I have
brought my father's tobacco and
my grandfather's beer.  Between
their tombstones, I light a sparkler
and *(with eyes open)* imagine them
standing and dancing before me.
So I get up and dance with them,
turning, spinning, and falling to the
ground.  As I catch my breath, I look
up to see their smiles shine down
like porcelain stars.  They point at me.
"There's our boy; he's come to
drink and smoke with us.  He loves
the lost ones with a heart as big as
heaven and inhales our graves as if
they were fields of red roses."

The beer widens my eyes, makes
the deep night opaque.  Revealing
a tribe of dead lovers who protect
us from devils and demons, insuring
our first communions and last rites,
ready to welcome us back home
with cold soft hands.

The graveyard is full.  The living
and their dearly departed sit in tight
family circles telling old stories that
recall ancestors whose names have
now been given to babies.

We pass funeral cards, rosaries, and
wedding rings among us – tiny monuments
to people whose portraits hang along the
stairs leading to the cellar where we make
our candles, crush hot peppers, and shed
our tears.

We slice lemon cake, eat chicken breasts,
and drink tequila in the Cemeterio de Santa
Rosa.  The ghosts are all brown, except mine.
Pale faces who've passed over – German,
pot-bellied, serious white people, who,
in life, had things to accomplish.

We sing and dance to all the dead gone.
Mock death and remember a cast of bit
players who slip into our dreams with
whispers just before dawn.

As I pour my tequila into the earth, I see
their spirit mouths open and skeletons
rise to dance three feet above the ground.
White vapor swirling like clouds. Sweet
misty blankets that embrace the tombs
of my family.

**Charles P. Ries**

**First Kiss**

We leaned against
the side of her house,
in the only spot of
shade on the
entire farm.

We had been ordered
outside to
"Get some fresh air."

Beige dust swam
in the thick rays of
a late July sun.
Scratchy sepia pollen floated
up from the moat of
wheat fields surrounding her
house, cart-wheeling
on the air across the
gravel road
to that
wedge of shade

where we leaned,
our small spines
pressed against the cool white stucco,
reenacting the scene from
"Guiding Light"
that her mother had
just clicked off before
shooing us, reluctantly, outside.

I played Mike Bauer
and she was Elizabeth Spaulding,
lovers separated by
his recent faked death
and her current husband.

She said to me,
"I love you Mike Bauer."
Then she shifted,

her little lips
pushing against mine.
I could feel
the lines of her teeth
beneath the pink flesh of her pucker.

I didn't know
how to kiss back.

She moved her head
away from me,
brown pigtails bobbing
side-to-side as
she told me,
"That wasn't how
the real Mike Bauer
kissed Elizabeth Spaulding."

**Amy Henry Robinson**

## The Man Who Hated Cities

moved to a small town
which rapidly became a city
and moved to a smaller town
which began to become
a bustling city
and moved out to the edge of town
but the edge grew populace
and nearly became another city
and moved farther out
to the edge of the edge
which immediately started to grow
and become another city
and moved even farther out
to the edge of the woods
which were quickly being developed
and moved into the woods
among the darkening trees
and saw some hunters
and moved back farther
into the deepest part
of the already over-
crowded woods
and finally found
a cave in the side
of a hill deep
in the darkest part
of the woods
and lit a fire
which cast his shadow
on the walls of the cave
in the hill in the
darkest, deepest
part of the woods
and put out the fire
because now he knew
that it wasn't cities
or towns or crowded
woods or shadowed caves
that he hated
it was people
even himself
his own
shadow

**E. M. Schorb**

## The Souls

Outside on a green lawn a giant water-oak conducts a sunset.
   Some unsteady hum has summoned us out of our houses.
My ancient lady friend, who lives nearby, is jawing now and wears
   an awed-holy expression as she says they are souls, yes sir.
And they are everywhere, they wade the dusky clouds, they are
   giant black-winged fruits hanging, falling, bouncing. The green
is black with them. And neighbors stare; they worry for their

cars and pickups. If they get into the red berries, it's hell on
   paint. Shoot them. No, they are beautiful. They are a menace.
Look out below! They rise and wheel, kaleidoscopic, inside rings
   of themselves. They set themselves against the sky, black on blue.
They caw. They are telling themselves, or us, something.
   They caw and caw, and what is it they are saying, so
earpiercingly, holes through your eardrums, through your brain,

as if lasered? Then they settle again, like a black blizzard
   of huge coal flakes. The souls come back to visit us to tell
us that they know everything now. Now their sharp yellow beaks
   pierce the lawn. They are busier than worms in a feast
of famishment, an ecstasy of appetite. Now, she says,
   the nonagenarian, I'll soon be with them, and then
it's always now for me like them. The souls have found their

bodies. I don't know which is which, but somewhere, there,
   is everyone who died, all the loved ones, and even the others,
the ones that nobody loved. They are all there now, she says.
   I stare as deep as I can see. They are every blessed
place—on roofs, looking down, in trees, on bushes, under,
   over, and around. Some seem to be waiting, some tug
at the turning-emerald lawn in the lowering light: and now

how do they know to rise suddenly and become one wide
   black wing? How do they know to circle and circle in unison,
one boomerang black wing composed of so many blood-beating,
   sky-rowing black wings? How do they know when it's time
to fly along a horizon, rimmed with rising red? The souls,
   they know, they know! I think it must be out of some distant
folklore that the old lady speaks, eyes fixed, waving them goodbye.

E. M. Schorb

## Big Cats and Saxophone

We met across the distance of counties
in a spell of break-ups, unemployment,
and disappointment.  She would drive close
to one-hundred-and-twenty miles to reach my door.
She ignored the alcohol on my breath,
found her way between my sheets
before her shoes could leave her feet.

She asked me one morning
that if we went to a zoo
what exhibit I'd take her to first.
"Big cats" I answered.  "No question about it,
the pumas, the jaguars, the tigers."
That apparently was
the right answer as I felt her crawl
on top of me in the dark.

She played jazz saxophone in a band,
though she never played for me.
She said she practiced at a zoo
and park near her apartment.
She was stable, sweet and horny,
but my life was about to implode
so I let her fade.

Sometimes I still imagine her, practicing,
working the keys, mere feet away from
something that paces inside the iron bars,
elegant, deadly, the color of a sunrise,
the perfect note echoing into the
man-made caves, the lush, pagan scrape
of pacing claws.

**Troy Schoultz**

## Cosmic Weather

The Red Hurricane on Jupiter
first stirred before a man learned how to strike flint in those caves
where sweat tasted the dark sun of sacrifice and gristle.

The Red Hurricane
began its churning before the hammering of bronze, the usage of bitumen
to pave streets lined with citadels of glazed brick, while a bald scribe
stylus-tallied an inventory of wheat, clay pots of mead, gold ingots,
and slaves.

Mornings, dusks on Earth, tides pregnant with the moon, harvest of
olives, birth of stones, and honing of birds' song from noise to the
grammar of a great thirst, while the Red Hurricane, ammonia shrapnel
& Richters of methane, gyre'd.

The Red Hurricane:
crimson-gouged eyeball of Cyclopes, skinned testis of a black bull
pierced by a hundred banderillas, while here on earth tribe decimated
tribe, and Baal smoked on the plains of murder.

And later,
when a priest officiated before a snake goddess clutching serpents in
her fists, breasts jutted, her dress frilled with jabots of combustion,
the Red Hurricane began to spin in an atmospheric pressure so dense a
square inch would vaporize that faience idol.

And much later,
when the farmer of Hellas recited hexameters of benched ships and
betrayal, the hurricane would rotate up into one hemisphere, then down
again, sweeping distances, rotations lasting hundreds of years.

Generation begot generation, fields were cleared, corpses were burned,
and galleons embarked, flotillas treasured with lice and smallpox,
argosies oozing dysentery, ships circumnavigating the globe, while
mace'd fists bore wax-sealed papacies, Dystopias, new Zions, quetzal
feathers, ash.

And the Red Hurricane,
all thrust and compression, persisted. Tenochtitlan fell, yet the Red Hurricane persisted.
Lisbon shook, Catholic marble bludgeoned rosaries, and the hurricane persisted.
Monsoons and drought, locust swarms, yet the Red Hurricane endured, a sanguine yolk
waxing.

And when the 20th century opened, with the sky now harnessed and New Mexico
sand smelted in the furnace of a split atom, the Red Hurricane spun and swelled.

Weather on Jupiter remained—by terrestrial standards—apocalyptic:
gas clouds bled electricity into radiation tsunamis, atoms sweated
electrons, and the air hardened to a metal at its core

     because that hurricane had not settled,
nor will it for hundreds of years, when slowly, very
slowly, at the velocity of tectonic plates ripping a continent in
two, sprouting granite mountains, the clouds will seal, and the storm
will dilute, samite sheets of hydrogen, rip-curls of electricity.

     While on earth,
entered above a strata of fossilized crustaceans and fern,
a strata of reptiles,
one of mammals with bones as delicate as violin strings,
one with the litter of arrowheads, re-bar and oil;
man and woman will be
imprints in sandstone – a species crusted in
rock, petrified and
buried beneath a barren steppe of absence and heat.

**Anthony Seidman**

## Dream World

I look toward my mother's bed
in its sunny spot by the window.
Her young nurse is smiling.
So is Mother.
She lies in a blue hospital gown,
a geometric print of triangles, squares and circles,
in shades of gray, burgundy and dark blue.
Her skin looks healthy.
Her thin white hair is brushed off her face.

After the nurse leaves, she asks,
"Do you want to play bridge? We need a fourth."
Her eyes are wide and bright.
"I haven't played in years," I say.
She accepts that excuse
and points her painted nails
to the others she imagines in the room.
"They will play," she says.

I stroke her damp forehead,
holding her bony hand bruised from the needles.
I brush my fingers down her silky legs
now devoid of hair.
"Do I look a mess?" she asks.
The setting sun casts a shadow across her bed.
"No, you look wonderful," I say.
She smiles, not minding
that her mouth is without her bottom dentures,
and brags how her cousins
tell her how good she looks
and how well-dressed she is.
Even here with her gown hiked up to her diaper,
she cares how she looks.
I try to pull her gown down.
She keeps grabbing it.
I cover her with a sheet
and sit down to watch her play cards.

"Six spades," she says.
"Play out." I play out.
She uses her nightgown as her bridge hand,
trying to lift off each pattern section,
one by one as if it were a card
and place it on an imaginary
table in front of her.

I want to know what happened to her
and what can be done about it.
"Hospitalitis," the nurse says.
She has seen it a million times before.
I go back to the bed and continue play-acting.

I am thankful too.  Her mind is taking her
to that other place where she is young and
beautiful and lives on the west side of Chicago.
I haven't seen her so happy in years.
"I like this little room," she says.
"I'm glad," I say.

**Madeline Sharples**

## I Asked My Love

I asked my love to lie with me last night,
his face appeared unchanged, his smile the same:
this morning I rose early with the light.

At his approach I felt the air ignite,
he whispered softly: spoke my secret name.
I asked my love to lie with me last night.

He said my eyes seemed older, he was right:
only the dead remain immune to change.
This morning I rose early with the light.

His lips touched mine as in a holy rite,
his touch seared through me like a sacred flame.
I asked my love to lie with me last night.

I trembled as our breath became one breath.
He brought me to a place beyond all pain.
This morning I rose early with the light.

He went from me just as the sky grew bright.
I called my love.  I called my love by name,
I asked my love to lie with me last night.
This morning I rose early with the light.

**Eileen Sheehan**

## Water Planet

"The death of the oceans means the death of man."
                                          Jacques-Yves Cousteau

Now we've seen it
                from space:
green granite continents,
rolling galaxies of charted
water, salt depths
forging the birth and
death of man in a wet blur.

Despise what nurtures.
Take cyanide and dynamite
to coral, monofilament
drift-nets to salmon and squid.

Repeat the
                'no-one's looking'
Anthem of the River Slavers,
bury waste and death
in the source of life.

Put the resurrection engine
of the world into overdrive,
harvest piled bones gone
to chalk on Antarctic beaches.

Raw stone eyes
                of thalidomide bass
netted off New Jersey's coast
stare through tricolored haze.

A sea's no God
to endure everything.

Or is, and dies before us.

Dies with gliding dolphins
cast like leaves,

hardens to a snow of petro-
chemical rosebud ash
                leaving only massive
tube worms and blossoming
magma rifts
on the deep sea's
desert floor.

**Michael Shorb**

125

## Round Dance

Men and women, one by one,
dance until the dance is done,
along the hallway in the glass,
reflections within those who pass
on courses similar to their own
to places where they love alone,
with big red noses, custard pies
and a pair of sightless eyes.

Men and women, two by two,
dance until the dance is through
and when the lack of music palls
move furtively through unlit halls
to where each lover stoops above
the promise of romantic love,
the big red nose, the custard pie
and the hard enamelled eye.

Men and women, three by three,
dance until it's *tout finis*
and though they feel a little grief
the passage down the hall is brief,
a second's searching for the light,
a moment's love, then empty night –
the big red nose, the custard pie,
all in the twinkling of an eye!

Men and women, four by four,
dance until they can no more
then slowly from the floor repair
towards the steep, unlighted stair,
where, as they silently descend,
darkness awaits them at the end
with big red noses, custard pies
and a shade across his eyes.

Men and women, five by five,
dance pretending they're alive
or at the tables of small bars
pour alcohol onto their scars
until at last all their dejections
become as comic as affections,
with big red noses, custard pies
and a pair of painted eyes.

Men and women, six by six,
dance until they've had their fix
and all that sparkles is profound
until the lights stop turning 'round
and you hear, "That's all, folks.
another of life's little jokes,
with big red nose and custard pies
and a knife to peel the eyes."

Men and women, seven by seven,
dance into their seventh heaven,
jiving through the offertory,
faces lit in stained-glass glory,
to where the ancient bobby-soxers
lie in long black wooden boxes,
with big red noses, custard pies
and photographs of Old Blue Eyes.

Men and women, eight by eight,
dance until the night grows late,
when lashes at which young love pines
run down the cheeks in greasy lines
and lips that tempted once now drool,
though eager still to play the fool
with big red nose and custard pies
and sockets where there should be eyes.

Men and women, nine by nine,
dance until the fiddles whine
for all the passion that has faded
in halls where love once masqueraded,
for all the passageways of lust
that have been buried in the dust
with big red noses, custard pies
and with bright lascivious eyes.

Men and women, ten by ten,
dance from the cradle yet again,
along the hall to dancing class,
from the small bar to Sunday mass,
with feelings out of all proportion
to love and romance and abortion,
with big red noses, custard pies
and a pair of condemned eyes.

**Raymond Southall**

**Frankfurt Airport**
(for Debbie Wright)

Stopped over in this sterile air-con place
We sit, squeezed into soft plastic seats,
Gazing out the plate glass at idle jets
Nestled in quiet neon darkness
As the automatic walkway click-clacks gently,
Marking out the slow passage of time:
A dim metallic heartbeat
Reducing all thought and all memory
To the loose penumbra of unreality.

Airport jokes fade into dumb nothingness
As time stretches out to meet infinity
Somewhere high above the blank map of Germany;
And another airline rep smooth-talks us
Into accepting the extended waiting patiently.
Just a technical hitch, he says,
Smiling his vapid airline smile,
Reducing all feeling, all sensation
To numb inevitability.

I smoke one more cigarette and you sleep,
Your tousled head on my lap, your doll hand
Draped languidly in mine.
Almost not here, away in a hallucinating space,
A flickering smile plays upon your face:
You are Kali Ma, dancing the Earth to dust,
And I am The Perfumed Saint,
Exuding insufferable benign sweetness.

I press my ear to your red, full lips,
Listen to the slow rhythm of your breathing,
The hieroglyphs of your dreams,
The dark ocean of your being;
And through the torpid mist
Of this transitory soulless place
I sense the quintessential spirit,
The ineffable mystery that is you.

**Dee Sunshine**

128

**Taking Possession**

The tumbler turned, the key withdrawn, the threshold crossed,
The house was empty, cold,
    scent of cigarettes,
Tattling of regular Friday night whist
And crinolines and big bands over the radio.

Rank kitchen drawer
Echoing with the roll of the abandoned
    corkscrew,
House of smoke and drink
And of successive husbands and habits.

You lit a match; the kettle went on.
Your arms wrapped me from behind,
    your body the shield
Between me and the spectres,
As slight and as lasting as their stench.

We climbed, found the garret,
Scarred our knees, our elbows,
    on the bare wood floor,
Our heat reassuring the ghosts
About the return of joy to the old timbers.

Soon after, you found a broom and swept the hearth.
I reached for the
    porcelain pot and,
Under the kitchen's jaundiced eye,
Put the tealeaves through their agony.

**Lois Swann**

## Thanksgiving

The frost left a simple beautiful pattern
      on the black car roof
Like stars clustered or marcasite
      threaded with silver.

Shivering, undressed, I find such marks sparkling
      on the skin of my inner thigh,
The sign of you I am loathe to bathe away,
      fearing to squander diamonds.

**Lois Swann**

## Voyeur

She's like expensive candy,
hard to unwrap.
I watch you struggle slightly to open her
from my vantage point
in your black office chair.
You don't appreciate her utter perfection:
narrow hips, small breasts and silence.
You lean back on our bed
with your sea-blue pajama pants
hanging half off your waist
and wait for her to become useful.
She is high and eager but you
force the yield,
knowing it tortures me.
You place her in your lap and begin—
one hand on her neck,
pushing her down to our satin sheets.
She yelps as you pay her no mind,
already on auto-pilot
away in some distant jungle
where cavemen still roam.
You leave me cold
yet you're a hundred degrees,
heaving, sweating and staring at me.
You want to make sure I see
as you finish with her.
You rise up, knees on either side of limp hips,
and breathe that smile of victory
over both of us.
You've worn her dry
and now the lady sleeps
soaked in you.
I gag;
the scent of you so thick in the air
it wraps me in its sick blanket.
Trails of your infection crisscross our mattress
and create a sticky, white web of damnation
as my hands find my stomach to trace the
memories of you that burn across it.
You begin to sing her a lullaby
in a voice that reminds me of a Greek chorus
full of aborted choir boys.
It's a brutal mouth forming beautiful words.
I want to kill her.
You never sing for me.
I turn to run, to escape our cave,
but I am hunted down in the hallway
and, with the taste of her
still on your lips,
eaten alive.

**Julie M. Tate**

## The Lost World

No one speaks the words I need to know.
The name of the tree near the Ventura mission
that lopes and lurches like a drunken dragon
when the wind blows, exposing a sinewed belly
of branches, or the name for when you see the tree
from your car and lower the radio
as if to hear it better, wishing you could
stand still in the street as the car continued
without you, into town, obeying each empty light.

I don't know the words for the wildflowers
that orgasm in this vacant lot, though they've coaxed
my tears with their yellow fingers, their violet mouths.
No one speaks the names of the four-petaled blue compass
or the golden clarinet that turns a man into
a honeybee, and few know. Though any child
will tell you the name of the blinking towers on the hill
or two roads crossing, no one knows
the word for crying and laughing at the same time,

or the verb for two people thinking the same
thought in the same moment—and variations
when it occurs with your lover on a cross-country trip
and you thought she was asleep; another name
when it rises in bed as she dips her chest
into the mirror-water of your face; another word
when you stand together in the kitchen,
slicing carrots and peppers and turn toward each other
in the same instant, and nearly knife each other,

and you start laughing and you do not speak
the thought, because it is everywhere like breath,
like protons, and you know lightning has struck you both,
but also everything—the room, the world. And it is
another thing entirely when you are with your dad
sitting on a mildewed wicker couch in a dark room,
and he is dying, and for a moment you both glow
remembering talks in the woods at night—a flash
of divine mercy, another name no one speaks.

Sam Taylor

## The Undressing Room
### for Asha Greer

They all had to stand naked there
all ages in front of each other
women, children, and grandmothers—
sunken and budding breasts
      side by side, as if
      each was alone in a room of mirrors

placed at different angles and dates,
reflecting one body through every age,
what she once was, what she might have been,
an illustrated life of the soul's anatomy
      depicted with variances
      for childhoods and chestnut trees,

bowls filled with pears or peas,
a stern father who played the violin,
a kiss beneath the steps of a forbidden
church, all facing the same fate.
      And each knew the feel of the rain
      in the ground beneath their feet,

each was a witness to the brain, each could
recite some text from memory,
the sting of a bee, the call of a lark,
a flint-spark off the heart.  Except each stood
      half-atrophied,
      as if the present moment had worn through

every fantasy.  In truth, they were not alone—
they were packed like herrings in a tin.
Yet each had to answer for herself
the same question:
      How will I meet my death?
      Will I shriek?  Will I scream?

Will I lift up one of the children
and hold her to my chest?
Will I sing?  Many of the women sang.
Though there was no reason to sing
      around them were no birds prattling
      in bowers, no milk and honey to bless

just naked bodies and souls squirming
from their defects in the last, unfriendly light
before an asphyxiated death.
Still some sang. They sang for something else,
      something that would not perish
      and had not even been touched

by the gloved hands and secret orders,
the early morning box cars rolling slowly
out of Bialystok through the beech flowers.
That's when the woman telling me
        the story paused and almost smiled
        and came again from a different angle.

*Maybe there never is a reason,* she said.
I didn't know if she had been there.
She wouldn't tell me, she said it didn't matter.
I knew at least she hadn't died.
        *Maybe that's the question we answer*
        *each moment of our ordinary lives.*

In line at the bank, buying milk for the night,
in traffic fumes and ice-sleet storms, siren-breathed:
how will I meet my death?  How will I
meet my death?  And maybe there never really is
        *a reason*
        to sing

even in the arms of our beloved, wife or husband,
even when we're licking
a coconut sno-cone or chocolate torte,
walking into a movie with our popcorn
        or driving, window-sealed, through the poor
        side of town, where a black girl turns

and slaps us with a look.  How will we
meet our death?   . . . And the boys and men
entered that room too, undressed, and squirmed.
Would their humiliation really be
        their last concern?  Would they still pretend
        not to cry?  Some screamed.  Some held

a hand.  And like the women, many of the Rabbis
sang.  Was it that stripped to the bone
they chose to wrap themselves in that clothing?
Or was it that, stripped of everything—
        their clothes, their names, their lives—
        that's what was left, they were, the singing.

**Sam Taylor**

### Aunt Julia's lover

You giggle & twist your shoulders for the photographer trying to catch
your yearbook smile in 1930. At seventeen, your face is an unlocked window
in the moonlight, a waltz, a whisper of passion under the smile of a sailor's
arms, alongside your mother's cherry tree where school days slid off your
shoulders. The pearl button falls from your blouse – with your soft voice onto
the grass. Somewhere deep inside a drawer I have the silver spoon you saved from
*The Palmer House Hotel.*

I imagine this tryst, a stolen rendezvous with the sailor – spent holding
hands across a linen table, how he must have carefully unfolded the lavender
starched napkin onto his lap & later unfolded you under the sheets while you
watched a piano playing secrets in his eyes, waiting for the rest of your life to
begin in that single afternoon.

A husband, a house, a baby carriage, a life that never came true, staring
in the mirror, angels at your side – it doesn't work to close the years in your eyes.
You never found the map for lost lovers, children or lives. You died before you
were born, in a glass room, darkly.

I imagine you now, a ghost of a girl, silky blushing blue as you swan into
the pale city streets at night, searching for your past life to wander a world of
hallways & rooms inside *The Palmer House* where you & your sailor lover once
slept. Folding back warm sheets still damp & twisted, you feel a familiar soft sush
across your cheek as his fingers touch your face. You look up to see the threshold
of his smile, a flashing snap of bright light that lifts & carries you up and into a
wedding of forever.

**Arlene Tribbia**

## The Rescue of Natalie Wood

She plays the victim so often,
her small shaky voice
seems as tiny as she is,
those beautiful dark Russian eyes pleading
like rippling pools of fear . . .

And now she is here –
in this dark water –
no camera to record her fear,
no sound engineer
to capture her cries . . .
just a curious moon
spreading no light
as her slim form slips
almost imperceptibly
beneath the surface.

I wait in the cold current,
then surge forward,
grabbing her.

She's so fragile,
doll-like almost.
I can barely make out
her perfect features
in this troubled seascape.

I hold her firmly,
her face just above the wave.
We struggle in the darkness,
no ship's light,
no miracle lifeboat,
no compass, no guide . . .

I hold her tightly,
our breathing labored.
I hear her whispered prayers
like soft billowing epiphanies
carrying us  quietly  gently   safely
back to shore.

**Vernon Waring**

## A History of Red

Lifted out of the horrific flames of Hellfire
by God's bare hands, that first red, molten

vermilion dripping through his fingers, might explain
the sun and Mars, specks of now cooling stars.

To offset the persistence of green in the Garden, red
poured over tomatoes, radishes, raspberries, fuchsias,

roosters and cardinals, a mere streak across the fleet
blackbird's wings, a tinge in the legs of shrimp,

vivid again in snappers, cochineal anemones and coral
in warm oceans.  After a blush of shame, the same shade

as the apple when those two were caught red-handed,
came menses, Abel's blood, Ham's wine harbinger of clarets,

burgundies and port, Cleopatra's henna-stained lips,
rubies and garnets on the death masks of pharaohs,

the rusty sea Moses led the chosen through, russet
autumn maples.  Later, clay bricks, fireworks in China,

clerical robes, Titian's models, rouge, the color spreading
like plague in scarlet fever, rashes, sanguine flags,

Little Red Riding Hood, a 50/50 chance in roulette, jackets
at fox hunts, boiled lobster, communists, hot peppers, geraniums,

the flush of rubella, what we see when we're angry,
ruddy complexions, cerise British buses and telephone boxes,

a lighted district of prostitutes, kidney beans, a new penny,
cinnabar, the coppery skin of the Navajo, valentines,

poppies for the fallen in battle, failure to show a profit,
crimson lipstick, ketchup, fire trucks and hydrants, stop signs,

bureaucratic delays, a railroad porter's cap, Coke labels,
Matisse's magenta studio, algae tide, Tabasco, distress flares,

Grenadine, early morning plane flights, paprika, traffic signal,
auburn hair, maraschino cherries, Crane's badge of courage,

cranberry glass, exit signs, international hospital crosses, and
the terrible wounds of war even now somewhere in the world.

**Sarah Brown Weitzman**

Painter

Looking at bug guts, mostly yellows and greens, through the windshield
or eating watermelon under the delicate pink of a dogwood
with a cardinal hopping in and out of puddles of sun on the grass,
we can imagine God as a painter

working with a limited palette, a trinity at first,
his blue period lasting eons for over-brimming oceans and skies
while fire, blood, bursts of hot lava, and the excesses
of sunsets soon used up red, just drips and splatters left for geraniums

and apples. While daubing forsythias, egg yokes and flitting canaries,
had he overturned yellow into the cistern of left-over blue
so then green green green poured out onto the grass, leaves
and the fruits he couldn't wait to let ripen for his still lifes?

A minimalist phase would account for redwing blackbirds,
luna moths and stripped skunks. What an eye for detail
in black dots on the ladybug's wings, the eyes of the panther at night,
the bow after rain. Even shadows release purple tints

the impressionists discovered. So many colors, such variety,
almost nothing was left untouched, though he'd have had to miss
a few which would explain angel wings, clouds, wave crests,
albinos, and Carara marble because he never managed the climb.

A general lack of restraint in some patterns and shapes shows in
the rococo of jungles, tropical fish, bird plumage, and the baboon's rear.
If he had a grand design, he obviously revised it on alternate continents and
in a fury, like an ice age, smashed up everything a couple of times.

I suppose he finally gave up on this canvas and is off now
somewhere in the universe starting fresh, looking back at us
over his shoulder just past Uranus, saying, "Oh, that,
that was when I was just learning."

**Sarah Brown Weitzman**

## Flying White

With the dampened fine point
brush of long-bristle horsehair,

he deftly snatches some carnelian
red with quick flicks of the wrist

as if plucking rice with chopsticks.
He funnels a life's worth of technique

and insight into practiced strokes,
dabbing, grazing, feathering

the rice paper, circling, circling.
Not perfect, thank goodness, but

not bad for a persimmon, with tracks
of bare paper in between the paint,

an effect in sumi-e called "flying white,"
here to thread the fruit with highlights.

The pressure he applies must be just
so, or harsh and broken lines are left.

He is pleased, but not too pleased,
sets aside the brush, picks up the tea

his wife left him who remembers when.
Out on the deck, he leans on the bamboo

railing, sips, watches in the sky a plane
shedding vapor trails across a setting sun.

**Philip Wexler**

## Hard Drive

Coming down from the floor
above, she penetrated my strapped
quarters on the pretext of trouble-
shooting my computer.  I offered
her a chair but she declined, so
I reclined as she wedged herself
between me and the machine,
bending over parabolically in her skin
tight jeans, screwdrivers, pliers, can
of lubricant sticking out of her
back pockets, cold metal touching
the naked ribbon of her waist.
She was so close that her behind,
hardware and all, rubbed up
against my knee, and I didn't shrink
from the contact, on the contrary,
nor did she, whose forceful tapping
on the keyboard filled the monitor
with line after line of the word "MORE."
I sensed an itch and hardened
my heart against it, to no avail.
It was time to advance to the power strip.

She reached back to bring my hands
to her waist where they rubbed
and kneaded while she poked
and stroked the mouse, propelling
the cursor in a pulsating trajectory
across the screen.  I inched a hand up
the right side of her stretchy red blouse.
She pressed "SHIFT."  I slid my other
hand under the left side.  Another
"SHIFT."  With both hands, I reached
way under and up her bulging
front.  She chucked away her tools
and dropped onto my lap.  Pliant
as a contortionist, she extended
a bare leg over the keyboard
and with pink-painted toe pressed
"ENTER," or was it "INSERT?"
And who was I to deny her anything.
Turbocharged, we rose to peak
performance under the desk.  Relieved
and satisfied that all systems
were in order, we disconnected
and entered sleep mode
for the duration.

**Philip Wexler**

140

**Night of Down**
(Berlin - November 9, 1938)

The feathers, the down, more
than anything else, I remember.

People, these days, they talk only
about shattered glass, official havoc,

sanctioned confusion, an incessant
din. Yes, maybe

I heard some breaking, shouting,
faintly from the main streets.

But the neighbors that dropped by
without knocking spoke little, broke

no glass. The clatter they made pulling
out drawers and overturning tables was faint.

Softer still were the sounds of the quilts,
blankets, and pillows they ripped. This part

they carried out with great spirit.
They were like children, shaking fluff

throughout the rooms, down stairs,
and out the windows. It was a soft falling

snow, and I could see it snowing
out the windows of other houses.

In my life I never thought
about the insides of our bedding,

but that night, after we gave up
pleading with them to stop,

we stood aside, spectators,
and I mourned

the slaughter of all the ducks and geese
we ever ate. This scattered plumage,

their coats in life, was the filling
we slept on and under, while we stuffed

their bodies other ways
so we could gorge our own. Such fowl,

supporting us with their lives.
Our neighbors shook hands

for a job done rightly, and left.
No stormtroopers these, just simple folk.

Once the blizzard settled, my husband
leaned his forehead against the cold

kitchen window, his eyes shut.
My son I released from the foyer closet

and he ran about tossing
the white stuff over his head.

I sat on the floor in a drift,
feeling what it is to be plucked

when there are no more
feathers to give.

**Philip Wexler**

## Potato Salad

At the picnic, Mom
shoved Rita's face
into the potato salad,

and told her to keep
her hands off Dad.
It wasn't all that

difficult, the salad
maneuver, I mean.
She tilted the bowl up

with her right hand,
cupped her left
on Rita's flaming

red hair and, quite
ladylike, slapped
the two together.

A shallow, vague
impression of a face
was left

in the potato salad
still clinging
to the shiny steel bowl.

I'd never seen Dad
speechless before.
Rita slapped him

for not coming to her
defense, as if it were
possible.  Afterwards,

Mom carried on
like nothing happened,
peeling the cellophane

off the sweet potato pies.
Taking no chances,
everyone inched back,

and Aunt Esther tried
to drag me away.  Mom
was smiling, but had

no more mischief
on her mind.
Still wiping potato

salad from her face
and slyly licking some
(it was so darn good),

Rita glared at her,
and sped off
in a flaming red

sports car.  Dad shrugged
his shoulders and went
into the woods to smoke

his pipe.  Awkwardly,
people began leaving.
Small though I was,

I escaped Aunt Esther's
clutches, and helped
myself to a ladleful

of the potato salad
imprinted with, yes,
Rita's flaming red lips.

**Philip Wexler**

## Their Morning in Flannels

He sits at the table screaming.
She stands at the stove scrambling.

He asks for answers, reasons.
She dices, sprinkles spices.

He is spitting mad, glares.
She fries and trembles, cries.

He accuses, fumes, threatens.
She denies, pleads, gets out the plates.

She takes the offensive, ridiculing,
pressing for confessions, motives.

He defends, rebuts, deflects.
She throws down the silverware,

tells him to get his own damn juice.
His neck tightens, turns red.

She brings the omelet to the table and sits.
"It needs more salt, Cynthia, as usual."

"Oh, Jim, let's put it aside." She touches
his shoulder. Tentatively, they kiss.

A solitary woman pauses outside
the window, latches onto the momentary

kiss, thinks how lucky they are,
how she longs for such a life.

She resumes walking. In the kitchen
they wave knives at each other.

Philip Wexler

## Under the Weather

Fresh out of the shower
you sit down opposite & I wonder
at the one brazen drop, the runaway
tearaway bead sneaking down your cheek –
meeting co-conspirators at the ear lobe
      abseiling to the slowly rising nipple
         then joyously plummeting
to the soft springs of pubic hair.

You don't understand the cause of my wonder
but that's okay because we've been naked like this
beyond count, sometimes
beyond interest,
but we always return to this certainty of flesh.

I follow the path of those drops like their lowliest acolyte;
my tongue repeating their paths of prayer.

Hand paints in broadest strokes,
moving in to fine point/
the detailing of arousal.

You always say this is a dance,
demanded rhythms beyond timing.
Seeking deepest resonance
where the music itself moves with you.

But to me we are painting –
the coaxing of colour from
beneath the white canvas of our skin.

My hands are moving hard, avoiding the tender points
but nudging flesh towards those centres
as if your whole body was congregating.

Your hands are roving lightly
like a bay-protected tide.
You reach down & surprise us both
(because in these things we can all
be at the edges of extremity).  A few words
& you come out to greet these two fingers.  I
come in like a boulder easing into earth.

We seek the rhythms of your dance.  Blood rushes north,
rushes south.  My thumb
grinds nipple to fine ochre/
you are so intent

& have come, then try to come again but I miss cues
(as usual, imagination beats the art) –
have to wind down

to a calm, so calm that lakes are left looking
strung out & shabby/
              stillness poured from a distillation of afternoon sun/
                       a book waiting in its store – gilt, ink & resin.

We sense a rhythm in the distance
as though initially it has nothing do with us:
something in the flat downstairs even
a movement deep in the earth.
Both concentrating,
trying to find a point where it meets & seconds us.

It does.
This pulse is neither smooth, nor subtle.
You can't call it any relative
of waltz or bossa nova.
This is a storm.

Your hands are busy again,
a slickened finger slipping in
stirring frenzy in the spine.
Then you
then me.

I lie on you.
Like moon-teased water you rise again from time to time –
those aftershocks you love.
*Just . . . yes . . . .*
I move & am still simultaneous.
*Just like this.*

**Les Wicks**

## Citrus

flat moonlight on the great wide mesa
        contains in its brilliance a circular idea
of full moon the snowfields of other places
        glistering with irised ice on humped and
smooth plains full of shadow and always a cold
        interminable silence growing deeper the
deeper you listen until you are there at
        two citrus trees near the plaza where
for some mysterious reason the birds all noisily
        choose to congregate in the gray dawn when
luminescence is barely there as the eyelid of
        the sky cracks open on the eastern horizon far
against the *Sangre De Cristos*   a wild matin of
        many high pitched tiny voices stabbing out of
the round dark heads of the trees not yet able to
        be seen as green as though a small bomb has
burst out of the darkness and its shrapnel is
        sharp obsidian shards that you hear rather
than see or feel and are not sure they even
        exist   thinking for a moment it must be
the trees themselves making this litany to a
        powerful star

        until after sunrise
they are perfectly green and silent and tourists
        step carefully around chalk-like droppings
painting the red brick walks at their base
        not knowing all the notes that have flown
leaving small white husks which are nothing more
        than wild grains mixed with morning

**Daniel Williams**

## The Old Italians of Aquatic Park

the old men of Aquatic Park
sit on hard wooden benches
late in the afternoon
their eyes moving left, right
front, center as if at a tennis match
pausing to feed the pigeons
using their hands like cutting knives
to separate the crust from the bread
which they toss into the air
like rice at an Italian wedding
rising to brush the crumbs
from their baggy trousers
one with a suit vest and tie
pulling at the gold chain
holding his pocket watch
tucked securely next to his heart
the old men of aquatic park
have the smell of garlic and pasta
embedded in their skin
Italy beating in their hearts
the old men of aquatic park
are dying off with grace and dignity
and a love for the old ways

there is something sad
about being Americanized
there is something sad
about growing old
the bocce ball rolls slowly
along the grass lawn
coming to rest like a hearse
parked next to an open grave
funerals wait on them
flowers scattered like empty promises
the mourners growing fewer in number
their ranks depleted
file slowly into their cars
disappear into the shadows
of late afternoon monotony
bocce ball will resume
in the morning
there are pigeons to be fed
wine to drink, stories to tell
the thirst for life masked in the
face of death

**A. D. Winans**

## The Blessed

I wake up happily beside your back,
Its naked shoulderblades as near as dusk.
They sway ever so lightly as you breathe—
A motion imperceptible did I
Not know so well the rhythms of your body.
You're sleeping; I can hear the whisk of breath
From out your nose—the quiet rush of warmth
Warming your upper lip (perhaps a bead
Of moisture lingers there)—it sounds just like
The sighing of a distant breeze!  So quiet . . . .
To think that sound could be so quiet, and yet
Be heard!  Or is it my imagination?
Perhaps I am so rapt that I imagine . . . .
Your hair is knotted on the pillow, tangled
In piles tickling my lips, which kiss
The strands in bunches (since their counterparts
Upon your face—though longing to be kissed—
Are turned away and inaccessible).
Clichéd it is, but . . . I inhale your hair.
It is a kind of secret, guilty pleasure,
Which I permit myself occasionally.
And then I touch your back, a timid finger
Afraid to mar the skin, which looks as if
It's made of fairy-tales solidified.
How can there be such symmetry in life?
—Except . . . yes, I see an auburn fleck
On one side of your back, right near your neck.
It's almost hidden by the hair; to touch
It I must move the tousled mass aside
—Though slowly, carefully.  You mustn't wake.
Who knows what dreams are passing underneath
Your darting eyes (for surely they are darting,
Bird-like, as I have seen them do before).
Oh, how I'd like to see your face right now!
A glimpse only . . . perhaps of just the dimple
That bunches up the right side of your face
(It's deeper than the other, prettier).
Or maybe just your lips—or your eyes,
Those sapphires that I sometimes dream about.
But I must lie here restlessly, in rapt
Anticipation of the moment when
You'll wake.  To look into your droopy eyes,
To be the being they see first, as sleep
Still clings to them . . . .  Your sluggish smile will be
The answer to my expectant grin.  And then
Together we will sit outside, beneath
The dogwood tree, and watch the setting sun.

**Chris Wright**

150

## On the Loose

In traffic's wake he stands, shuddering,
silently bearing his cardboard entreaty,
while mute processions of unattached witnesses
head for destination anchors.

Unchained to any routine's desk,
unwanted by the taxman's agent,
ears free from cellular growth,
no lawn requires his cutting attentions.

No fashion's demands hold his body.
Divorced from scheduled grasp,
he holds a wealth of unblocked time
undreamt of by the passersby.

Unfettered and footloose,
no ties that bind or obligate,
addressed constraints unknown,
free to roam and choose his bridge,

yet tied to hunger's appetite
and ninety-eight point six,
to unrelenting sleep demands
and deep thirst's slaking,

to endless foraging hunts
for respites from the cold,
survival's endless demands
suck seconds from his life.

Shackles of want, chains of choice –
what a difference a lane makes.

**Martin Zehr**

## Bar Serendip

She snuck up behind him
like a panther in the dark
and draped herself around his neck
like a python around its next meal.

If he had looked into the mirror
like an owl into the night,
he would have seen her coming
as sly as a witch on a broom

but he was too busy talking
like a magpie in a tree
on how The Beatles ruined Rock
like Cortez ruined the Aztecs.

She was as drunk as a fish
flopping on a pier
and as beautiful
as a full whisky bottle

when her empty-glass voice
curled a thirsty question
around the dangling part
of his lusting left ear.

Her "Buy me a drink?"
flowed into his mind
like a river of gin
into a lime-and-tonic sea.

He smiled into her smile
like a vulture circling in the sky.
"Maybe," he said
like a bee buzzing into a rose.

"What's your name?" he asked
as if he owned all the flowers
that blossomed every night
in the garden of her thighs.

**Larry Ziman**

## Father Dancing

My father liked to dance alone.
Late at night, when he was sure
the rest of the house was sleeping,
he would turn on the old Philco
and dance with the broom.

One summer, when mother sent me
out with his lunch, I caught him
doing the rhumba in the berry patch.
Music seemed to come from his pores.
One winter, he waltzed for the cows.

I went to the barn to feed the cats.
I found him doing a perfect pirouette.
His arms spun out and up
until he was like a giant top
spinning before the stalls.

The cows were lowing into their cuds.
I could tell they'd seen it all before.
Occasionally he would spin to a stop,
bow, kiss one of them right on the nose,
and two-step back into his turning.

One day I caught him dancing nude
in the small meadow down past our creek.
He and the dance were exquisite as prayer.
I thought of Noah's sons covering
their father's nakedness, and wondered why.

**Fredrick Zydek**

## The Boy Who Lived on Perkins Street

He liked stamp and coin collecting over
sports, used the radio for only news and music,
preferred hiking through the woods to games
of tag and enjoyed Tarzan comic books

over *Mechanics Illustrated* and *True Detective*.
He didn't like guns, wouldn't go hunting
and found ways to get out of fishing because
he didn't like killing worms or hooking fish.

He liked to climb trees, bring in the cows,
feed chickens, gather eggs, chop kindling
and hang out in the kitchen when Grandma
baked cookies.   He liked churning butter,

keeping the spring on the Edison Victrola
wound tight when his uncle played Glenn
Miller and Harry James records and could
spend hours picking and eating fresh cherries

from all his favorite trees.  This was a boy
who favored books to pinups, and watching
clouds take on unexpected shapes to doing
homework.  It was difficult for him to be

on time for things. Tardy was his middle
name.  He said it was because he was always
dreaming and that whether people knew it
or not,  good dreams did not have deadlines.

Fredrick Zydek

## The Death of Plecostomus

For years he lived in the tank,
watching the filters darken,
nibbling plastic weeds, performing
magic for snails, clap-grass,
and one porcelain mermaid
blossom-deep in grains of sand.

He knew the tank like the eagle
knew the field, and he could swim
with such simple grace
sometimes truth grew a newer name.
I once caught him watching me,
wooing me back to the germ of man.

I gave a single pellet, a garland
for the skinny victory between us.
He took it as though to scratch its soul.
For one minute I almost believed
in the last mineral agony
of an all mineral thing.
Then, one night he swam too far.

I found him mute as a sponge,
bruised as an invalid plum
lying on the cold plastic
of the kitchen floor.
Had he bumped and gagged
through four rooms to find me?
I Knew the sting of fear along his bones

and rushed him back
to his fifty-gallon dream of escape.
He tried, once, to escape again, then moored
himself beneath some plastic kelp.
In the morning, he was belly up,
and the one-eyed Swordtail
had eaten most of his left fin.

**Fredrick Zydek**

## The House on A Street

It was a house where net sacks of onions,
wild hazelnuts and English walnuts hung
from wooden pegs on the attic's ceiling
to keep the mice from getting to them. We
kept a wood-burning stove in the kitchen
to check the chill of cool mornings, a few

chickens to ward off earwigs and bottles
of homemade root beer on the lee side
of the back porch to take in our lunches.
The house was always clean, the wood box
always filled with kindling, and the lawn
always trimmed and neat. There was an

upright piano in the living room, pump organ
in the hall, a squeeze box and two guitars.
It was a house where music took privilege
over politics and what my father called
*literary airs*. He kept rabbits in hutches
behind the garage. Mother called them

four-legged chickens when she fried them
for Sunday dinner. Ours was the finest
vegetable garden on the block and the only
strawberry patch for miles around. Dad
kept a rocking chair on the front porch
and a fishing pole and basket on the back.

Except for the few times he went downtown
to have a beer with his pals or play cards,
I doubt an hour passed in which he wasn't
trying his best to provide for us. I marveled
at how quietly and vigorously he cared, hoped
that someday I would be a man like that.

**Fredrick Zydek**

## The Line Dance of Field Ants

They're on safari again.  It happens
every summer.  The only thing that's never
sure is the direction.  One year they headed
west.  There was a carcass of a stillborn calf
at the end of that journey.  I don't know
if they were hauling back flesh or bits of bone.

Are ants carnivorous?  Perhaps they build
castles made of bone beneath the shelterbelt.
Maybe there are cities down there that would
make Frank Lloyd Wright swoon with envy.
How much winter do they get down there?
Who lights the halls I'm told they build?

Today they have headed south.  Somewhere
out there they've found new work that will
sustain them.  I will check daily.  Eventually
the line of ants will lead to strange and waiting
booty.  They will make their way to this find
until all that's left are bones or thistles.  Then

the dance will end with the last of them, prize
held in pincers, doing the rumba or watusi
as it carries a tiny spoil through the tiny door
that leads to their enormous city.  Inside
there will be feasts and celebrations.  Perhaps
lady ants will drape themselves in fine silks

and strut, slow and sexy, across some stage
where all the workers have gathered.
Perhaps there will be music and some kind
of ale.  Maybe there's a philharmonic down
there for all those ants who don't go out
to the fields, and great taverns with lady mud

wrestlers for those who do.  One thing's for
sure. The ants know something we don't –
how to go single file without crowding.

Fredrick Zydek

# Notes on Poets

**Chuck Augello** lives in Randolph, New Jersey, with his wife, his dog, his three cats, and a growing collection of dust. His fiction and poetry have appeared in *Rattle, The Santa Fe Literary Review, Pindeldboz, Word Riot, SLAB*, and other journals. He spends his days in a cubicle, slowly plotting his escape.

**Fred Bahnson** is the recipient of the 2006 Pilgrimage Essay Award, was shortlisted for the 2007 Lange-Taylor Prize from Duke Center for Documentary Studies, and was the William Raney scholar in non-fiction at Bread Loaf Writer's Conference in 2008. His poems and essays have appeared in *Orion, The Sun, Fugue, Geez, Pilgrimage, The Rock & Sling, Sojourners, The Cresset* and the anthologies, *Dance the Guns to Silence: 100 Poems for Ken Saro-Wiwa* and *Best American Spiritual Writing 2007*. He is currently a Food & Society policy fellow at the Institute for Agriculture and Trade Policy. He lives in Brevard, North Carolina.

**Gay Baines** has been writing since she was eight-years-old. Her work has appeared in *REAL, Rattapallax, Poet Lore, Nimrod, California Quarterly, The Pinch, dislocate, Louisiana Literature*, and many other journals. In 2008, she was awarded the Mary and Gil Stott Award for writing. She is co-owner of July Literary Press. At present, she is preparing a chapbook, *The Book of Lies*, for publication. She lives in East Aurora, New York.

**Kristin Berger** lives with her husband and two children in Portland, Oregon, where she serves as an Associate Editor of *VoiceCatcher*. She is the author of a poetry chapbook, *For the Willing* (Finishing Line Press, 2008), and her non-fiction has been nominated for the Pushcart Prize. Kristin's poetry and essays have appeared in *CALYX, New Letters, Mothering, The Pedestal Magazine*, and other publications. For more about her, visit her website at www.kristinberger.wordpress.com.

**John C Bird** has worked as a civil servant, journalist, and university lecturer. His poetry has been widely published in newspapers, magazines, and anthologies. His published and broadcast work also includes plays, short fiction, television comedy material, and non-fiction books on subjects as diverse as Britain's treatment of enemy aliens in wartime and new careers for the over-40s. His first novel, *Alby and Me*, was longlisted for the UK Waverton Good Read Award for the best debut novel of 2007-8. He lives near Birmingham, England.

**Regina Murray Brault** lives in Burlington, Vermont, where she leads the Cherry Lane Poet's Workshop. She received her diploma in the arts from Burlington College in 1997 at the age of 60. She previously served as editor of the *Mountain Troubadour*. She has judged local, national, and international poetry contests, and has served as critic for The League of Vermont Writers as well as the Poetry Society of Vermont. She is the recipient of over 250 national and international poetry awards, including the 2008 Creekwalker and the 2008 Euphoria poetry awards. Her poem, "At Either End of the Web," received a 2009 Pushcart Prize nomination. And her poem, "Timesweep Cantata," was a finalist in the Salem College Center for Women Writers 2009 International Literary Award Competition. She was named 2009 Vermont Senior Poet Laureate by Angels Without Wings Foundation. Her poetry has appeared in more than 90 publications including *Hartford Courant, Comstock Review, Grandmother Earth, Karamu, Northwoods Journal, Silver Quill, The Mennonite, Anthology of New England Writers, Ancient Paths Literary Magazine, ByLine Magazine, Crucible, Lyric, Midwest Poetry Review, Poet Magazine, Sacred Stones, State Street Review, Bloodroot*, and June Cotner's Random House anthology, *Mothers and Daughters*. Her first illustrated book of poetry, *Beneath the Skin*, was published by Jane Wollmar in October 2007.

**Susan Breeden** lives in Houston, Texas, and works as a technical editor for the aerospace industry. Her fiction, essays, and poetry have appeared in commercial and literary publications, including

*Woman's World, Playgirl, BorderSenses, Zone 3, 34th Parallel*, and *Texas Magazine* published by the *Houston Chronicle*.

**Don Brennan**, a retired high-school teacher, won the *Haight Ashbury Literary Journal* 1st Prize for Poetry in 2000, and he won the Milton Dorfman 3rd Prize in 2001. He has hosted and co-hosted numerous poetry readings including the Yakety Yak series, the Bibliohead Bookstore readings, and the Hospitality House readings at the San Francisco Main Library. He is widely published in journals and anthologies, including the City Lights 2007 anthology, *From the Other Side of the Post Card*. His books include six poetry chapbooks and a novel, *Barbaria*, released by PublishAmerica in 2009. He lives in San Francisco, California.

**Alan Britt** teaches English and Creative Writing at Towson University. His recent books are *Vegetable Love* (2009), *Vermillion* (2006), *Infinite Days* (2003), *Amnesio Tango* (1998), and *Bodies of Lightning* (1995). His work appears in the anthology, *American Poets Against the War* (Metropolitan Arts Press, Ltd., 2009) and in *Vapor Translantico*, a bi-lingual anthology from Hofstra University Press. He lives in Reisterstown, Maryland, with his wife, daughter, two Bouviers des Flandres, one Bichon Friese, and two formerly feral cats.

**MCBruce** is a lawyer in McKinleyville, California. He hosted "The Poets Café" on KPFK in Los Angeles and was the editor of *The Blue Mouse*. His chapbooks include *Clients* and *The Book of the Dead*.

**Howard Camner** is the author of 16 books of poetry and an autobiography, *Turbulence at 67 Inches*. He was the headliner with New York's West End Poetry Troupe from 1978-1981. He is recognized as Florida's most widely published poet and was nominated for Florida's Poet Laureate in 1980. He has received the MiPo Literary Award and was named Best Poet of 2007 in the *New Times* "Best of Miami" readers-poll edition. He lives with his wife and children in Miami, Florida.

**Carol Carpenter** has had poems and stories published in numerous online and print publications, including *Margie, Snake Nation Review, Neon, Georgetown Review, Caveat Lector, Orbis*, and in various anthologies such as *Not What I Expected* (Paycock Press, 2007) and Wild Things (Outrider Press, 2008). Her work has been exhibited by art galleries and produced as podcasts (*Connecticut Review* and *Bound Off*). She received the Hart Crane Memorial Award, the Jean Siegel Pearson Poetry Award, Artists Among Us Award, and others. Formerly a college writing instructor, journalist, and trainer, she now devotes her time to writing in Livonia, Michigan.

**Alan Catlin**, since retiring from his unchosen profession as a barman, has been working on various extended writing projects. His fictional memoir in progress, *Hours of Happiness*, is a series of linked short stories and a novel. Poetry projects include several chapbooks on art. Published titles include *Down on the Beach* (Snark Publications), *Our Lady of the Shipwrecks* (Finishing Line Press), *Effects of Sunlight in the Fog* (Bright Hill Press), *Self-Portrait As the Artist Afraid of His Self-Portrait* (March Street Press), *Men in Suits* (Madman Ink), and *The Insomniac's Gift* (Shark Art). He lives in Schenectady, New York.

**Joanne Riley Clarkson** has published two chapbooks of poetry, *Pacing the Moon* (Chantry Press) and *Crossing Without Daughters* (March Street Press). Her poems have appeared in many journals including *Emrys, Cimarron Review, South Dakota Review*, and *The Seattle Review*. After working as a professional librarian for 20 years, she re-careered as an RN with a specialty in hospice care. She lives with her husband in Olympia, Washington.

**Rob Cook** is the author of *Songs for the Extinction of Winter* (Rain Mountain Press, 2007), *Diary of Tadpole the Dirtbag* (Rain Mountain Press, 2009), and *Blackout Country* (BlazeVox, 2009). His work has appeared in *The Bitter Oleander, Colorado Review, Tampa Review, Zoland Poetry, A Cappella Zoo,*

*Fence, Greatcoat,* and others. He lives in New York City.

**Barbara Lydecker Crane** is a longtime quilt artist and a relative newcomer to poetry. Recent poems have been published or accepted by the *Christian Science Monitor, Light Quarterly, Measure, Four and Twenty, Raintown Review, Blue Unicorn, Lucid Rhythms, Bumbershoot,* and others. She is the founding member of "X. J. Kennedy & the Light Brigade," a small group of Boston-area performing poets. In 1995, she was awarded a New England Foundation for the Arts Regional Fellowship in Visual Arts. Her quilts (primarily landscapes) are in public and private collections, including the National Quilt Museum of the United States, the New England Quilt Museum, Cambridge Savings Bank, and Massachusetts General Hospital. She lives in Lexington, Massachusetts.

**Steve De France,** MFA, has traveled widely in the United States. On more than one occasion, he hitch-hiked across America. He rode the rails on freight trains, worked as a laborer with pick-up gangs in Arizona, dug swimming pools in Texas, did 33 days in the Pecos city jail as a vagrant, fought bulls in Mexico, and dove for salvage off a small island off the coast of Mazatlan, Mexico. His poetry has been published in most English-speaking countries. Recently, his work can be seen in *The Evergreen Review, The Wallace Stevens Journal, The Sun, Rattle, Why Vandalism,* and others. He has won writing awards in England and in the United States, and he continues to write poetry, plays, essays, and short stories. He lives in Long Beach, California.

**Stephanie Dickinson** lives in New York City. Her work has appeared in *Green Mountains Review, Gulf Coast, Short Story, Glimmer Train, Dirty Goat, Fourteen Hills,* and others. Spuyten Duyvil published her novel, *Half Girl. Corn Goddess,* a book of poetry, and *Road of Five Churches,* a collection of short stories, are available from Rain Mountain Press. Along with Rob Cook and the cats, Vallejo and Sally Joy, she edits *Skidrow Penthouse.*

**James Doyle** lives with his wife, poet Sharon Doyle, in Fort Collins, Colorado. His most recent poetry book is *Bending Under the Yellow Police Tapes* (Steel Toe Books, 2007).

**Nicola Easthope** lives with her partner and two-year-old daughter on the Kapiti Coast of Aotearoa, New Zealand. Before motherhood she was an English teacher and an advocate for Education for Sustainability while writing poetry to keep sane and happy. Her poems have appeared in *The Guardian* (UK), *The Red Wheelbarrow* (Scotland), New Zealand Poetry Society anthologies, *Landfall* (NZ), *Poetry New Zealand, Takahe* (NZ), and *Staples* (Australia). She won 2nd prize in the Bravado International Poetry Competition in 2005.

**Maureen Tolman Flannery** has had her work published in fifty anthologies and over a hundred literary reviews, recently including *Birmingham Poetry Review, Xavier Review, Calyx, Pedestal, Atlanta Review, Out of Line,* and *North American Review.* Her newly-released book of poems about Latin America is *Destiny Whispers to the Beloved.* Other volumes of her work include *Ancestors in the Landscape: Poems of a Rancher's Daughter* and *A Fine Line.* Although she grew up on a Wyoming sheep ranch, she and her actor-husband Dan raised their four children in Chicago. She now lives in Evanston, Illinois.

**Christine Fotis** has had her poetry published in *Page Seventeen, Litmus Journal, Seven Deadly Zines,* and others. She researched and compiled the updated edition of *Aussie Slang Dictionary.* As an editor for a small publishing company, she loves helping other authors create their best writing. She volunteers for *Harvest Magazine* and also works as a digital artist. She lives in Melbourne, Australia.

**Marilyn Friedman** lives in Los Angeles, California. Her poetry has been published in *Pearl, Squaw Valley Review, California Quarterly,* and *Rockhurst Review.* She teaches poetry and creative writing at Writing Pad, a school that she founded where gourmet food is served at every class.

161

**Cheryl Gatling** is a registered nurse in Syracuse, New York. A chapbook, *Stickley Wood*, is available from FootHills Publishing. Her poem "Schroedinger's Newspaper" can be seen and heard as a multimedia piece online at www.bornmagazine.org.

**Howard Good**, a journalism professor at SUNY New Paltz, is the author of nine poetry chapbooks. *Visiting the Dead* (Flutter Press, 2009) is his most recent. He lives in Highland, New York.

**June S. Gould**, Ph.D., is the author of *The Writer in All of Us: Improving Your Writing Through Childhood Memories* (E. P. Dutton, Plume). She also co-authored with Ruth Steinberg and Barbara Haber the poetry book, *Counting the Stones* (Shadow Press), and she now has a 2nd generation Holocaust novel, *In the Shadow of Trains*, from Xlibris. Some of her poetry has appeared in *The Writer's Round Table, International Women's Writing Guild, Dasein, Pearl, The Storyteller, Ship of Fools Press, SheMom, The Sheltered Poet, Talisman*, and *Inkwell Magazine*. She leads writing workshops and keynotes for The International Women's Writing Guild, The National Council of Jewish Women, The Aegean Arts Circle, and an Advanced Writer's Workshop at Shelter Studios in New York City. And she has received an award from the American Education Association for her written contribution to *Constructivism: Theory, Perspectives and Practice* (Columbia University Press). She lives in Fairfield, Connecticut.

**Nathan Graziano**, a high school teacher, is the author of three books of poetry, a collection of short stories, and seven chapbooks of poetry and fiction. His work has appeared in *Rattle, Night Train, Quercus Review, The Owen Wister Review*, and others. His latest book of poetry, *After the Honeymoon*, was published in 2009 by sunnyoutside. He lives with his wife and children in Manchester, New Hampshire.

**John Grey**, an Australian-born poet, playwright, and musician, is a U.S. resident since the late 1970s. He works as a financial systems analyst. He has had work recently published in *The Pinch, Ekphrasis, Cape Rock, Connecticut River Review, Rockhurst Review, Art Mag, Poetry East*, and *Reed*. He lives in Providence, Rhode Island.

**Rasma Haidri** is an American writer living on the arctic coast of Norway where she teaches English. Her poetry and essays have appeared in many journals including *Prairie Schooner, Runes*, and *Third Genre*. Widely anthologized, she has won the Southern Women Writers Association Emerging Writer Award in Creative Non-fiction, the Wisconsin Academy of Arts, Letters, and Science Poetry Award, the Mandy Poetry Prize, and other distinctions. More about her work can be found at her website, www.rasma.org.

**Joseph Hart** for the past forty years has been a founding member of Rutger's School of the Arts, creating ensemble theatre productions. He has now returned to poetry, his earliest love. He lives in Highland Park, New Jersey.

**Michael Hettich** has had his work published in numerous journals including *Orion, Prairie Schooner, Tri Quarterly, The Sun, Poetry East*, and the *Southern Poetry Review*. His books of poetry include *A Small Boat, Swimmer Dreams*, and *Flock & Shadow: New and Selected Poems*. He lives with his family in Miami, Florida, and teaches at Miami Dade College. Visit his website at www.michaelhettich.com.

**Kenneth Hickey** was born and lives in Cork, Ireland. After leaving Secondary School in 1993, he went to sea for seven years before returning to dry land to pursue a serious writing career. He set up the Will It Workshop at the Sirius Art Centre Cork where he regularly reads work in progress. He has read at the Frank O'Connor Festival and has had performances of several plays at various Cork Theatres. He has also had two rehearsed readings of full-length plays by Moving Parts Theatre at Carr's Café in Paris, France. His video shorts have been screened at the Cork and Foyle Film Festivals. Print publishing credits include *Southward 6* (the Munster Literature Centre anthology), *Destination Anywhere* (the Feel Free Press anthology), *Aesthetica Magazine, Shadow Poetry, Quill Magazine* (US), and others. He was shortlisted for the PJ O'Connor Awards and the South Tipperary Chapbook Awards in 2003 and 2004. And he won the Eamonn Kane Full-Length Play Award.

**Robert Hoeft**, a Northwest poet, lives and writes in Ashland, Oregon. Widely published in little magazines throughout the United States, he has also had poems published in Canada, England, and South Africa. His collected works include four chapbooks and one miniature book.

**Tom Holmes** is the editor of *Redactions: Poetry & Poetics*. He is also the author of *After Malagueña* (FootHills Publishing, 2005), *Negative Time* (Pudding House Publications, 2007), *Pre-Dew Poems* (FootHills Publishing, 2008), and *Henri, Sophie, & The Hieratic Head of Ezra Pound: Poems Blasted from the Vortex* (BlazeVox, 2009). His work has appeared online at *Verse Daily*. He lives in Brockport, New York.

**Tom C. Hunley** is an associate professor of English at Western Kentucky University in Bowling Green, Kentucky, and he is the director of Steel Toe Books. His books include *Octopus* (Logan House, winner of the Holland Prize), *My Life as a Minor Character* (Pecan Grove, chapbook contest winner), and *Teaching Poetry Writing: A Five-Canon Approach* (Multilingual Matters, New Writing Viewpoints Series).

**Lockie Hunter** teaches fiction, satire, and media/essay writing at Warren Wilson College in the hills of North Carolina. She is a graduate of Emerson College's MFA program in Boston, Massachusetts, and her poetry, fiction, and essays have found their way into numerous print and online journals. She is currently working on a low-country novel in hopes of preserving the eccentricities of her family and the region. She lives in Asheville, North Carolina.

**Marcia L. Hurlow** has had four poetry chapbooks published. Her most recent, *Green Man in Suburbia*, won the *Backwoods City Review* Chapbook Contest and was published last year. Her first book of poetry, *Anomie*, won the Edges Prize at Word Press. She lives in Lexington, Kentucky, and teaches creative writing, journalism, and linguistics at Asbury University in Wilmore, Kentucky.

**Carrie Jerrell** received her M.A. from the Writing Seminars at John Hopkins University. She received her Ph.D. from Texas Tech University. Her debut poetry collection, *After the Revival*, won the 2008 Anthony Hecht Poetry Prize and was published by Waywiser Press (UK) in November 2009. She is an assistant professor of English at Murray State University in Murray, Kentucky.

**Brad Johnson** is an associate professor at Palm Beach State College in Boca Raton, Florida. His two chapbooks, *Void Where Prohibited* and *The Happiness Theory*, are available from Pudding House Publications at www.puddinghouse.com.

**Amy Kitchell-Leighty** is a graduate of the Writing Seminars at Bennington College, and she teaches English at Vincennes University. Her work has appeared in *Bellevue Literary Review*, *The White Pelican*, *The Coachella Review*, and others. She lives with her husband and two dogs in Lawrenceville, Illinois.

**Jim Kober** is inspired by the solo work of guitarist John Frusciante. He lives in Tucson, Arizona.

**L. Leaf** has been writing poems most of her life but only occasionally made the effort to consider them closely for publication. Reading others' poetry supports and inspires the stories and novels she puts hours into every day. She lives in Chicago, Illinois, participates in writing workshops, and is part of the editorial staff of the *Chicago Quarterly Review*. Old Bean Hill Road in the Berkshires in Massachusetts is a pleasant route by day.

**Michelle Lerner** worked as a legal aid attorney for 10 years. She has an M.F.A. in Poetry from The New School. Her poetry has been published in *Lips, Paterson Literary Review, Harvard Women's Law Journal, Sojourner Magazine, Knock*, and many other print and online journals, as well as in the anthologies, *The Poetry of Place: North Jersey in Poetry* and *The American Voice in Poetry: The Legacy of Whitman, Williams*, and *Ginsberg*. She lives in Flanders, New Jersey.

**Lyn Lifshin** has had published more than 120 books and chapbooks of poetry. Texas Review Press published *Barbaro: Beyond Brokenness* in the Spring of 2009. In 2008, World Parade Books published *Desire*, and Red Hen Press published *Persephone*. In 2006, Texas Review Press also published *The Licorice Daughter: My Year with Ruffian*, a prize-winning book about the race horse Ruffian. *Another Woman Who Looks Like Me* was published by Black Sparrow Books at David Godine in 2006 and was selected for the 2007 Paterson Award for Literary Excellence for previous finalists of the Paterson Poetry Prize. Other books include *Cold Comfort* (Black Sparrow Press, 1997), *Before It's Light* (Black Sparrow Press, 1999-2000), *In Mirrors* (Presa :S: Press), *Upstate: An Unfinished Story* (FootHills Publishing), *The Daughter I Don't Have* (Plan B Press), *When a Cat Dies, Another Woman's Story, Barbie Poems, She Was Found Treading Water Deep out in the Ocean, Mad Girl Poems, Marilyn Monroe, Blue Tattoo, What Matters Most*, and *August Wind*. March Street Press brought out *A New Film About a Woman In Love* in 2003. Other titles include *92 Rapple Drive* (Coatalism), *Nutley Pond* (Goose River Press), *Light at the End, The Jesus Poems* (Clevis Hook Press), *Lost in the Fog* (Finishing Line Press), and Ballet Madonnas (Mastodon Dentist). She has won awards for her non-fiction and has edited four anthologies of women's writing including *Tangled Views, Ariadne's Thread*, and *Lips Unsealed*. Her poems have appeared in most literary and poetry magazines. She is the subject of an award-winning, documentary film, *Lyn Lifshin: Not Made of Glass*, which is available from Women Make Movies. An update of her Gale Research Projects Autobiographical Series, *On the Outside, Lips, Blues, Blue Lace*, was published in Spring 2003. *Drifting* is online. Visit her website at www.lynlifshin.com for interviews, photographs, more bio material, reviews, prose, and other samples of her work. She lives in Vienna, Virginia.

**Ellaraine Lockie** has seven published poetry chapbooks. She is the recipient of eleven Pushcart Prize nominations, the Lois Beebe Hayna Award from *The Eleventh Muse*, the Elilzabeth R. Curry Prize from *SLAB*, the One Page Poem Prize from the Missouri Writers' Guild, the Writecorner Press Poetry Award, the Skysaje Poetry Prize, and the Dean Wagner Poetry Prize. A non-fiction book author and essayist, she also serves as Poetry Editor for the lifestyles magazine, *Lilipoh*. She lives in Sunnyvale, California.

**Florence McGinn** has had over 400 pieces published, including free-verse poetry, essays, articles, haiku, and children's poetry. Her full-length collection of poetry, *Blood Trail*, was published in 2000 by Pennywhistle Press in New Mexico. Her haiku and free verse have been published in journals including *Midwest Poetry Review, Modern Haiku, Voices International, Paterson Literary Review*, and *Parnassus*. Her children's poetry has been published in *Cricket* and in *Clubouse*, and it has been used in McGraw-Hill's standardized tests, in the Montana Comprehensive Assessment System, and in the North Carolina Public Instruction Assessment. She has completed a novel manuscript. She presently serves on the New Jersey State Board of Education and served as a United States Commissioner on the US Web-based Education Commission during the Clinton administration. She is the retired Vice President of GKE (Global Knowledge Exchange) and has made presentations on innovative learning and the creative process throughout the United States and internationally in China, Australia, Italy, Singapore, Japan, and Korea. She taught English literature and writing for twenty-five years. She is the recipient of awards including US 1998 National Technology & Learning Teacher of the Year and the Princeton University 1998 Distinguished Secondary School Educator Award. She lives in Flemington, New Jersey.

**Michael McIrvin** is the author of five poetry collections including *Optimism Blues: Poems Selected and New*, the novel, *Déjà Vu and the Phone Sex Queen*, and the essay collection, *Whither American Poetry*. His new novel, *The Blue Man Dreams the End of Time*, was published by BeWrite Books in December 2009. He lives with his wife Sharon on the high plains of Wyoming.

**Terry Martin** is an English Professor at Central Washington University. An avid reader, writer, and editor of journals and anthologies, she has had published over 200 poems, essays, and articles. Her most recent book of poetry, *The Secret Language of Women*, was published by Blue Begonia Press in 2006. She lives with her partner in Yakima, Washington.

**Lorraine Merrin**, a Southwest native, now lives in the Pacific Northwest. Her work has appeared in various journals including *The Salal Review, Quercus Review, Rattle, Tar Wolf*, and others. She says, "Writing and breathing are the same. They sustain life."

**Les Merton** is linked to writing by words such as author, poet, dialectician, reviewer, competition judge, publisher, promoter, performer, and festival organizer. His penance for the forementioned sins is to be the founder and editor of *Poetry Cornwall*. He was made a Bard of Gorseth Kernow in 2004 for services to Cornish literature. His bardic name is Map Hallow (Son of the Moors). He lives in Redruth, Cornwall, England.

**Joyce Meyers** taught English in high school and college before becoming a lawyer. Her poems have appeared in numerous journals and anthologies, including *The Comstock Review, Atlanta Review, The Ledge, Pearl, White Pelican Review, Mad Poets Review, Philadelphia Poets*, and others. In 2004, 2007 and 2008, she received International Merit Awards from *Atlanta Review*. Her chapbook, *Wild Mushrooms*, was published by Plan B Press in 2007. She lives in Wallingford, Pennsylvania.

**Pamela Miller** has had three collections of poetry published, including *Fast Little Shoes* (Erie Street Press), *Mysterious Coleslaw* (Ridgeway Press), and *Recipe for Disaster* (Mayapple Press). Her work has appeared in many print and online journals and anthologies, including *The Paris Review, Pudding Magazine, Free Lunch, Wicked Alice, flashquake, Inhabiting the Body, Her Mark*, and *Online Writing: The Best of the First Ten Years*. She lives in Chicago, Illinois, and is working on a fourth book, *Miss Unthinkable*.

**Fred Moramarco** is the founding editor of *Poetry International*, published annually out of San Diego State University where he taught literature and creative writing for many years. His poetry and literary criticism have appeared in many magazines and journals, and a great deal of it can be found online. He is also artistic director of Laterthanever Productions (www.laterthanever.org), a small, non-profit, theatre company he started in San Diego in 2006. He lives in San Diego, California.

**Carmel L. Morse** earned her Ph.d. in English from the University of Nebraska, Lincoln. Her work has appeared in *Pudding Magazine, Fairfield Review, Darkling, Dana Literary Review, Nexus, Children, Churches and Daddies*, and several other journals. She is an Assistant Professor at the University of Northwestern Ohio in Lima, Ohio.

**Nora Nadjarian** has had published three collections of poetry and a book of short stories, *Ledra Street*, and she has won prizes and been commended in international competitions. Her work has appeared in journals and anthologies in Cyprus, Germany, India, Israel, New Zealand, the UK, and the United States. In 2009, her story, "And the Seven Dwarves," was a finalist in the Binnacle Sixth Annual International Ultra-Short Competition at the University of Maine at Machias. Her poem, "Flying with Chagall," was published in the anthology, *All of Our Lives*, which was edited by Sarah Shapiro and published by Targum Press. You can contact her by email at noranadj@logosnet.cy.net. She lives in Nicosia, Cyprus.

**Peter Nash**, when he was eight years old, noticed Ormsby's *Diseases of the Skin* in his father's medical library. Reaching high above him, he dislodged the book which fell to the carpet and opened to a photograph of a naked native of the Amazon rain forest sitting on a log. Both testicles were so swollen with elephantiasis that they rested on the forest floor. The shocked little boy vowed that he would become a doctor and cure the man. Peter's relatives on his mother's side were writers, reporters, editors, and novelists. In junior high school, Peter's English teacher, Miss Violet Walker, after reading his first essay, told him that he would become a writer. But he was committed to a life of medicine. Though he has been practicing medicine for forty years, the voices of Miss Walker and the writers in his family have never stopped whispering. Ten years ago he finally listened and moved to a rural community in Northern California where most mornings he writes. A semi-retired family physician who makes house calls in his pickup with his dog Henry, he occasionally helps his wife in the garden, boards horses, and participates in the Mattole Salmon Group whose goal is the restoration of the Mattole River. He has recently been published in *Snowy Egret, Passager, Camas, Off the Coast, The Labletter,* and *City Works.* His chapbook, *Tracks,* won the 2007 HOTMETALPRESS Chapbook Prize, and he was the National Award Winner of the 2008 *City Works Literary Anthology.* He lives in Petrolia, California.

**Ann Floreen Niedringhaus** is the author of two poetry chapbooks, *Life Suspended* (Poetry Harbor, 2003) and *Parallel to the Horizon* (Pudding House Publications, 2007). Her work has appeared in numerous journals and anthologies, including *The Comstock Review, Sojourners, Albatross,* and *Peregrine.* She writes in view of Lake Superior in Duluth, Minnesota, and receives inspiration from participants in poetry groups she co-coordinates at the St. Louis County Jail.

**Leonard Orr** is Academic Director of Liberal Arts and Professor of English at the Tri-Cities campus of Washington State University in Richland, Washington. He is the author or editor of thirteen books of literary criticism or critical theory. His most recent published books are *Joyce, Imperialism, & Postcolonialism* (Syracuse University Press, 2008) and *James's The Turn of The Screw* (Continuum, 2009). He was named the Lewis E. and Stella G. Buchanan Distinguished Professor of English (2005-2008). His poetry has appeared in many journals including *Black Warrior Review, Fugue, Poetry International, Poetry East, Natural Bridge, Isotope, Midwest Poetry Review, Pontoon, Rosebud,* and *Rocky Mountain Review.* His poetry chapbook, *Daytime Moon,* was published in 2005 by FootHills Publishing, and his full-length collection, *Why We Have Evening,* was published in 2010 by Cherry Grove Collections, an imprint of WordTech Communications LLC. He was a finalist for the T. S. Eliot Poetry Prize and the Blue Lynx Poetry Prize, and he was a semifinalist for the Floating Bridge Chapbook Prize and the William Stafford Poetry Prize. He has been a featured reader in many venues throughout the state of Washington, and he has led poetry workshops at the Burning Word Poetry Festival and elsewhere. He hosts the open-mic and featured-poet events at Washington State University Tri-Cities, and he served as president of the Washington Poets Association for three years. In recent years he has taken up painting abstracts and had his work featured in a solo-exhibition of fifty paintings in 2007. Both his poetry and painting utilize a similar aesthetic based in spontaneity, surprise, and passion.

**David Parke** is a hypnotherapist and life coach. His short story "Lessons in Hate" appeared in *Cantaraville,* Issue 9. He lives in New York, New York.

**Rae Pater** has had many poems published both online and in print. She lives in Christchurch, New Zealand, where she teaches adult literacy and tries to snatch spare moments for writing.

**Roger Pfingston** is a retired teacher of English and photography. He has been writing and publishing his poems since the early 1960s. Much of his work these days can be found online in e-zines such as *Mannequin Envy, Poetry Midwest, Innisfree Poetry Journal,* and *The Pedestal.* His poems have also appeared in two recent anthologies from Iowa Press: *Say This of Horses* and *75 Poems on Retirement.* His most recent chapbooks are *Earthbound* (Pudding House Publications) and *Singing to the Garden* (Parallel Press). He is the recipient of an NEA Creative Writing Fellowship for his poetry and two PEN Syndicated Fiction Awards. He lives in Bloomington, Indiana.

**Ronald Pies** is the author of a collection of poems, *Creeping Thyme* (Brandylane), and a collection of short stories, *Zimmerman's Tefillin* (PublishAmerica). A physician, he teaches at Tufts University and at SUNY Upstate Medical University. He lives in Lexington, Massachusetts.

**Kevin Pilkington** is a member of the writing faculty at Sarah Lawrence College, and he teaches a workshop in the graduate department at Manhattanville College. He is the author of six collections of poetry. *Spare Change* was the La Jolla Poets Press National Book Award winner, and *Getting By* won

*The Ledge* 1996 Poetry Chapbook Competition. *Ready to Eat the Sky* was published by River City Publishing as part of their new poetry series, and it was a finalist for an Independent Publishers Award. His poetry has appeared in many anthologies including *Birthday Poems: A Celebration*, *Western Wind*, and *Contemporary Poetry of New England*. Over the years he has been nominated for four Pushcarts and has appeared online at *Verse Daily*. His poems and reviews have appeared in numerous magazines including *Poetry*, *Ploughshares*, *Iowa Review*, *Boston Review*, *Yankee*, *Hayden's Ferry*, *Columbia*, *Greensboro Review*, *North American Review*, *Gulf Coast*, *Valparaiso Review*, and *Urthkin*. He lives in New York City.

**Lucas Pingel** is an assistant professor of English at St. Catherine's University in Minneapolis, Minnesota. He is the author of two chapbooks of poetry, *The Storm That Killed the Tree* (Pudding House Publications, 2008) and *All Types of Breath Included* (Further Adventures, 2009).

**Patricia Polak** is enrolled in the Creative Writing Master's Program at Manhattanville College. Her work has appeared in or is forthcoming in *Baby Boomer Birthright*, *The Cape Rock*, *The Griffin*, *Karamu*, *Meridian Anthology of Contemporary Poetry*, *Poet Lore*, *RiverSedge*, *The South Carolina Review*, and *Wisconsin Review*. She has traveled in Europe, North Africa, and the Middle East. For two years she lived abroad in Eastern Europe and Russia. A native New Yorker, she lives in Manhattan with her husband, a historian.

**Connie Post** served as the first Poet Laureate of Livermore, California, 2005-2009, during which time she created two popular reading series, "Ravenswood" and "Wine and Words." Her poetry has appeared in *Calyx*, *Kalliope*, *Cold Mountain Review*, *Chiron Review*, *Comstock Review*, *DMQ Review*, *Dogwood*, *Iodine Poetry Journal*, *Main Street Rag*, *RiverSedge*, *Tipton Poetry Journal*, *Up The Staircase*, *The Toronto Quarterly*, and *Wild Goose Poetry Review*. She was the winner of the Cover Prize for the Spring 2009 issue of *The Dirty Napkin* and the winner of the 2009 Caesura Poetry Awards from Poetry Center of San Jose. She lives in Livermore, California.

**Julie Preis** lives in Silver Spring, Maryland. Her poems have appeared in several print and online publications. Her interests include children, old people, family relationships, low-effort cooking, travel, and learning Spanish.

**Doug Ramspeck** directs the Writing Center at The Ohio State University at Lima, Ohio. His poetry collection, *Black Tupelo Country*, received the 2007 John Ciardi Prize for Poetry and is published by BKMK Press (University of Missouri – Kansas City). March Street Press published his chapbook, *Where We Come From*.

**Charles P. Ries** is the author of five books of poetry and a novel based on memory, *The Fathers We Find*. His narrative poems, short stories, interviews, and poetry reviews have appeared in over two hundred print and electronic publications. He has received four Pushcart Prize nominations for his writing. Most recently he was awarded the Wisconsin Regional Writers Association "Jade Ring" Award for humorous poetry. He is the former poetry editor for *Word Riot*, Co-Chairman of the Wisconsin Poet Laureate Commission, and a former member of the board at the Woodland Pattern Book Center. He is a founding member of the Lake Shore Surf Club, the oldest fresh-water surfing club on the Great Lakes. He lives in Milwaukee, Wisconsin. Visit his website at www.literaiti.net/Ries/ for samples of his work.

**Amy Henry Robinson** is currently in Santa Monica, California, cleaning her oven instead of writing as she ought to. Her work has been published in *Origami Condom*. Her published children's book, *Too Many Monkeys*, is illustrated by her sister Janet. She loves her husband because he loves the cats.

**E. M. Schorb** has had his work published in *The Sewanee Review*, *The Yale Review*, *The Chicago Review*, *Carolina Quarterly*, *The Virginia Quarterly Review*, *The Texas Review*, *The American Scholar*, *Stand* (UK), *Agenda* (UK), *The Notre Dame Review*, *Rattle*, *The New York Quarterly*, and others. His poetry collection, *Time and Fevers*, won a *Writer's Digest* Award for Self-Published Books in Poetry, and it was also a 2007 recipient of an Eric Hoffer Award for Excellence in Independent Publishing. Another collection, *Murderer's Day*, was awarded the Verna Emery Poetry Prize and was published by Purdue University Press. His novel, *Paradise Square*, was awarded the Grand Prize for Fiction from the International eBook Award Foundation at the Frankfurt Book Fair in 2000. His latest novel, *Fortune Island*, was published in 2009 by Cherokee McGhee Publishers. He lives in Mooresville, North Carolina.

**Troy Schoultz** has been writing and publishing poetry, fiction, reviews, and articles for the past ten years. He recently earned a Master of Science degree in English from the University of Wisconsin at Stevens Point. Currently working on his first novel, he lives in Marshfield, Wisconsin.

**Anthony Seidman** is the author of several books and chapbooks, including *Combustions* (March Street Press) and *Where Thirst Intersects* (The Bitter Oleander Press). His poetry and translations can be found in such journals as *Beyond Baroque, Borderlands, The Bitter Oleander, Nimrod*, and *Skidrow Penthouse*. He lives with his wife, poet Estrella del Valle, and his children in Los Angeles, California.

**Madeline Sharples** has worked most of her professional life as a technical writer, editor, and grant writer. She currently is a proposal manager turning engineering "writing" into readable prose. She co-authored *Blue Collar Women: Trailblazing Women Take on Men-Only Jobs* (New Horizon Press, 1994), a book about women in non-traditional professions, and she co-edited the poetry anthology, *The Great American Poetry Show*, Volumes 1 and 2. She wrote the poetry for two photography books, *The Emerging Journey* and *Intimacy*, and she recently had poems published in *Memoir (and), The Muddy River Poetry Review* and *Perigee - Publication for the Arts*. "Lunch," an excerpt from her memoir in poetry and prose, *Leaving the Hall Light On*, also appeared in *Perigee*. Visit her blog, Choices, at www.madeline40.blogspot.com, where she posts poems, photos, and musings about life choices. She lives in Manhattan Beach, California.

**Eileen Sheehan** lives in Killarney, Ireland. Her work is featured in *The Watchful Heart: A New Generation of Irish Poets*, edited by Joan McBreen and published by Salmon in 2009. Her collections of poetry are *Song of the Midnight Fox* (Doghouse Books, 2004) and *Down the Sunlit Hall* (Doghouse Books, 2008). She is the current Poet in Residence with the Limerick County Council Arts Office.

**Michael Shorb** writes frequently about environmental and political issues in tones ranging from lyrical to satirical. His poem, "Water Planet," is dedicated to Jacques Cousteau, the pioneer ecologist. His work has appeared in numerous magazines and anthologies, including *Nation, Michigan Quarterly, The Sun, Poetry Salzburg Review, Rattle*, and *Underground Voices*. He lives in San Francisco, California.

**Raymond Southall** has written critical works including *The Courtly Maker* (Barnes & Noble), *Literature and the Rise of Capitalism* (Lawrence & Wishart), and *Literature, the Individual and Society* (Lawrence & Wishart). His poems have appeared in various collections including *Secrets Beneath Stones, Sailing in the Mist of Time, Across the Bridge, Traveling*, and *The Argument from Desire*. He lives in Wollongong, New South Wales, Australia.

**Dee Sunshine** is a new-age gypsy, poet, and artist. After writing this blurb, he is going to Spain to walk the Camino de Santiago. After that he might return to India. You can follow his adventures at www.facebook.com/captainmelted, and you can read more of his poetry at www.thunderburst.co.uk.

**Lois Swann** has written two novels, *The Mists of Manitoo* and *Torn Covenants*, both published by Charles Scribner's Sons and reprinted by Avon Books. *The Mists of Manitoo* also had a Dutch edition. She won the Boehm Memorial Prize for poetry, and she founded Calliope's Chamber, an ensemble of live music and live readings of her published work and works-in-progress. She lives in Cummaquid, Massachusetts.

**Julie M. Tate** works as a journalist and freelance nurse. Her writing has appeared in numerous literary journals such as *Papyrus* and *Cram*. She is the owner, author, and editor of Gossip [&] the Devil, a creative/lifestyle blog that features interviews with independent artists in a variety of mediums and also features commentary on the arts, culture, music, and travel. Her first chapbook, *The Rough Chronicles of Bipolar Romance*, is available through her publishing and design label, Modern Orphan Designs. Currently she is at work on a book of flash fiction. She splits time between Tulsa, Oklahoma, and Chicago, Illinois.

**Sam Taylor** has had poems published in many journals including *The New Republic, Orion, Agni*, and *Michigan Quarterly*. His first book of poetry, *Body of the World*, is available from Copper Canyon Press. He is also the lyricist for the band, Some Say Fire, whose website is www.somesayfire.com. He lives in Charlottesville, Virginia.

**Arlene Tribbia** is an artist who has had short stories and poems published in many print and online literary journals in the United States and Canada. Her short stories have been nominated for a Pushcart Prize, and she recently completed a novel, *The Ten Thousand Loves*. She lives in Palm Harbor, Florida. Her website is: www.arlenetribbia.com.

**Vernon Waring**, a native of Philadelphia, has a background in journalism, advertising, and graphic arts. His poetry has appeared in many literary publications including *The Writer, The Iconoclast*, and *Anthology*. His work has also been featured online in *Ascent Aspirations Magazine, Starving Arts Literary Magazine, poetic inhalation*, and *A Prairie Home Companion*. He lives in King of Prussia, Pennsylvania.

**Sarah Brown Weitzman** grew up in Port Washington, New York. Over 200 of her poems have been published in many magazines such as *Poet & Critic, Ekphrasis, Nassau Review, North American Review, American Writing*, and *Potomac Review*. She received a National Endowment for the Arts Fellowship and twice was a finalist in the Academy of American Poets' First Book Award. In 2003, she was a finalist for both The Foley Prize and the National Looking Glass Poetry Chapbook Contest. Her second chapbook, *The Forbidden*, was published in 2004 by Pudding House Publications. A full-length volume of her poems, *Never Far from Flesh*, was published by Main Street Rag in 2005. Retired, she now lives and writes in Delray Beach, Florida.

**Philip Wexler** has had over 80 poems published in assorted literary magazines through the years and has given readings of his work in the Washington, D.C. area. He lives in Bethesda, Maryland, where he works for the Federal Government.

**Les Wicks** has had work published in over 200 different magazines, anthologies, and newspapers across 12 countries and 7 languages. His 9th book of poetry is *The Ambrosiacs* (Island, 2009). He lives in Mortdale, New South Wales, Australia.

**Daniel Williams** has been writing poetry of the Sierra Nevada in Northern California for 20 years. His work has appeared in many journals and anthologies. He has read at Cody's Books and Barnes & Noble, and he regularly records for KSER Radio in Seattle, Washington. When not writing of the natural world, he "vacations" in the 19th Century and finds many fascinating subjects for his poems there. He lives in Wawona, California.

**A. D. Winans** was born and raised in San Francisco, California, where he now lives. He returned from Panama in 1958 to become part of the North Beach scene. He is the author of over 45 books and chapbooks of poetry and prose, including *North Beach Poems, North Beach Revisited*, and *The Holy Grail: The Charles Bukowski Second Coming Revolution*. His poetry has been translated into 8 languages. He edited and published Second Coming Press for 17 years, publishing many Beat and post-Beat poets such as Charles Bukowski, William Everson, Lawrence Ferlinghetti, Allen Ginsberg, Bob Kaufman, Josephine Miles, Harold Norse, David Meltzer, and Jack Micheline. In 1980, he produced the Second Coming Poets and Music Festival, honoring poet Josephine Miles and blues-legend John Lee Hooker. In 2005, a song poem of his was performed at New York's Tully Hall. In 2006, he was awarded a PEN National Josephine Miles Award for excellence in literature. And Presa :S: Press published his *Selected Poems: The Other Side of Broadway* in 2007.

**Chris Wright** is a graduate student in history and philosophy in Boston, Massachusetts. His first book, *Notes of an Underground Humanist,* is available at Booklocker.com.

**Martin Zehr** is a clinical psychologist in private practice in Kansas City, Missouri. He is a member of the Mark Twain Circle of America and has made presentations on a number of Twain-related topics at regional and national literary conferences and at the international conferences on Mark Twain studies held in Elmira, New York, where the Clemens family spent their summers. His poetry has been published in *ZITIG*, the European online journal of culture and politics, and in the *Kansas City Star*.

**Larry Ziman** says, "Putting thoughts and feelings on paper without craft may be fun but never art." He lives in West Hollywood, California.

**Fredrick Zydek** is the author of nine collections of poetry. *T'Kopachuck: The Buckley Poems* was published by The Winthrop Press in 2009. Formerly a professor of creative writing and theology at the University of Nebraska and later at the College of Saint Mary, he is now a gentleman farmer when he isn't writing. He is the editor for Lone Willow Press. His work has appeared in *The Antioch Review, Cimmaron Review, The Hollins Critic, New England Review, Nimrod, Poetry, Prairie Schooner, Poetry Northwest, Yankee,* and others. He is the recipient of the Hart Crane Poetry Award, the Sarah Foley O'Loughlen Literary Award, and others. Retired, he divides his time between his home in Omaha, Nebraska, and a working corn-and-soybean farm in Brunswick, Nebraska.

# Acknowledgments and Permissions

Chuck Augello: "A Short History of Imperialism" is printed herein by permission of Chuck Augello.

Fred Bahnson: "Que Dios le Bendiga" first appeared in *Rock & Sling,* Volume 2, Number 2, Fall 2005, and is reprinted herein by permission of Fred Bahnson. "This Is How" first appeared in *Rock & Sling,* Volume 2, Number 2, Fall 2005, and also appeared in *Dance the Guns to Silence: 100 Poems for Ken Saro-Wiwa,* edited by Nii Ayikwei Parkes and Kadija Sesay, and published by Flipped Eye Publishing with African Writers Abroad in London in 2005. "This Is How" is reprinted herein by permission of Fred Bahnson.

Gay Baines: "Yankee Lake" is printed herein by permission of Gay Baines.

Kristin Berger: "Vanishing Point" first appeared in *Pilgrimage,* Volume 32, Issue 1, 2007, also appeared in her chapbook, *For the Willing* (Finishing Line Press, 2008), and is reprinted herein by permission of Kristin Berger.

John C Bird: "The Professor" first appeared in *Waves,* the annual anthology of the Society of Civil and Public Service Writers' Poetry Workshop in the UK, and is reprinted herein by permission of John C Bird.

Regina Murray Brault: "At Either End of the Web" first appeared in *Ancient Paths,* Issue 15, 2009, was the winner of the Euphoria 2008 Poetry Competition and appeared on its website, was nominated for a 2009 Pushcart Prize, and is reprinted herein by permission of Regina Murray Brault.

Susan Breeden: "Process of Elimination" is printed herein by permission of Susan Breeden.

Don Brennan: "Amtrak Overnight" and "Oolong" are printed herein by permission of Don Brennan.

Alan Britt: "The Old Toad" is printed herein by permission of Alan Britt.

MCBruce: "Travels with Jack" is printed herein by permission of MCBruce.

Howard Camner: "Doing Interstate 27" first appeared in his poetry book, *Brutal Delicacies* (Camelot Publishing Company, 1996), and is reprinted herein by permission of Howard Camner. "My Mentor" first appeared in the anthology, *PZ/Fort Point Special Arts Project* (Red Sun Press, 2000), and is reprinted herein by permission of Howard Camner.

Carol Carpenter: "To My Daughter on a Fine Fall Day" first appeared in *ELF: Eclectic Literary Forum,* Volume 2, Fall 1992, was reprinted in 2007 in the anthology, *Family Pictures: Poems & Photographs Celebrating our Loved Ones,* and is reprinted herein by permission of Carol Carpenter. "Wicker Chair & Coreopsis" first appeared in *Underground Window,* Volume 2, Number 11, November 2005, was reprinted in *Soundzine,* February 2009, and is reprinted herein by permission of Carol Carpenter.

Alan Catlin: "Iron" and "No-Tell-Motel Ship of Fools" are printed herein by permission of Alan Catlin.

Joanne Riley Clarkson: "Fire Mare" and "The Sin Not Taken" are printed herein by permission of Joanne Riley Clarkson.

Rob Cook: "Micronauts" first appeared in *Pearl*, #37, 2007, later appeared in his poetry book, *Diary of Tadpole the Dirtbag* (Rain Mountain Press, 2009), and is reprinted herein by permission of Rob Cook.

Barbara Lydecker Crane: "Alphabet Stupor" is printed herein by permission of Barbara Lydecker Crane.

Steve De France: "Hello, Out There ..." is printed herein by permission of Steve De France.

Stephanie Dickinson: "Ditch" first appeared in *Columbia Poetry Review*, No. 15, 2002, and is reprinted herein by permission of Stephanie Dickinson. "Iowa" first appeared in *Runes*, Gateway Issue, 2001, and is reprinted herein by permission of Stephanie Dickinson.

James Doyle: "Second Base on the Banana Boat" is printed herein by permission of James Doyle.

Nicola Easthope: "Watching you sleep . . ." first appeared in *Learning a Language*, the New Zealand Poetry Society's 2005 anthology, was commended in the NZPS International Poetry Competition in 2005, and is reprinted herein by permission of Nicola Easthope.

Maureen Tolman Flannery: "Lay the Sod o'er Me" first appeared in *JAMA*, Journal of the American Medical Association, May 23/30, 2007, under the title, "Take Me to the Green Valley," later appeared in *Ilya's Honey*, Fall 2007, and is reprinted herein by permission of Maureen Tolman Flannery. "Two Step" first appeared in *The Larcom Review*, April 2002, later appeared in *Curious Rooms*, 2002, also appeared in her poetry book, *Ancestors in the Landscape: Poems of a Rancher's Daughter* (John Gordon Burke Publisher, Inc., 2004), and is reprinted herein by permission of Maureen Tolman Flannery.

Christine Fotis: "Mittens" first appeared in *Litmus Journal*, Issue Minus Two, 2005, in Melbourne, Australia, and is reprinted herein by permission of Christine Fotis.

Marilyn Friedman: "Insatiable" is printed herein by permission of Marilyn Friedman.

Cheryl Gatling: "Even the Nails in the Sheet Rock Missed Her" first appeared in *Rattle*, Volume 10, Number 2, Winter 2004, was later reprinted in *Rattle*, Volume 12, Number 1, Summer 2006, "Tribute to the Best of *Rattle*," and is reprinted herein by permission of Cheryl Gatling.

Howard Good: "For the Woman Who Walked out During My Reading" first appeared in *The Orange Room Review*, April 2008, and is reprinted herein by permission of Howard Good.

June S. Gould: "Visit from My Mother on My Birthday" is printed herein by permission of June S. Gould.

Nathan Graziano: "A Frat Guy on a Motorcycle" and "Two Girls in a Tub Together" first appeared in his poetry book, *After the Honeymoon* (sunnyoutside, 2009), and are reprinted herein from *After the Honeymoon* by permission of sunnyoutside.

John Grey: "Thanksgiving at Jill's House" is printed herein by permission of John Grey.

Rasma Haidri: "The Last Photograph of My Father" first appeared in *Fish Stories*, Collective IV, 1998, and is reprinted herein by permission of Rasma Haidri.

Joseph Hart: "White Hole" is printed herein by permission of Joseph Hart.

Michael Hettich: "Loons" first appeared in his chapbook, *Singing with My Father* (March Street Press, 2001), and is reprinted herein by permission of Michael Hettich.

Kenneth Hickey: "This Love" is printed herein by permission of Kenneth Hickey.

Robert Hoeft: "The Day Everybody Went on Strike" is printed herein by permission of Robert Hoeft. "The Departure" first appeared in *Event* (Journal of the Contemporary Arts), Volume 12, Number 1, 1983, later appeared in his chapbook, *What Are You Doing?* (Trout Creek Press, 1987), and is reprinted herein by permission of Robert Hoeft.

Tom Holmes: "Chromolingustics" first appeared in *The Centrifugal Eye*, Volume 4, Issue 2, May 2009, and is reprinted herein by permission of Tom Holmes.

Tom C. Hunley: "How You'll Know You've Met Your Future Wife" is printed herein by permission of Tom C. Hunley.

Lockie Hunter: "Robinson Crusoe" first appeared online in *Opium Magazine*, and is reprinted herein by permission of Lockie Hunter. "Some Things My Sister Left Behind" first appeared online in *ken*again*, Winter 2006/2007, and is reprinted herein by permission of Lockie Hunter.

Marcia L. Hurlow: "To What Habit Do You Attribute the Longevity of Your Marriage?" is printed herein by permission of Marcia L. Hurlow.

Carrie Jerrell: "Big Daddy" first appeared in *Subtropics*, Spring/Summer 2009, later appeared in her poetry collection, *After the Revival* (Waywiser Press, 2009, UK), and is reprinted herein by permission of Carrie Jerrell. "Plainsong" first appeared in *The Eleventh Muse*, 2006, later appeared in *After the Revival*, and is reprinted herein by permission of Carrie Jerrell.

Brad Johnson: "Mall of America" first appeared in somewhat different form in *Chiron Review*, Winter 2008, and is reprinted herein by permission of Brad Johnson. "Married Saturday Mornings" first appeared in *New Zoo Poetry Review*, 2006, and is reprinted herein by permission of Brad Johnson. "The Wake" by Brad Johnson first appeared in *Thin Air*, Winter 2008, and is reprinted herein by permission of Brad Johnson.

Amy Kitchell-Leighty: "Our Gas Has Been Shut Off" is printed herein by permission of Amy Kitchell-Leighty.

Jim Kober: "This Is Not My Stop" first appeared online in *Ducts*, Issue 17, Summer 2006, later appeared in *Problem Child*, Volume 19, Issue 2, and is reprinted herein by permission of Jim Kober.

L. Leaf: "Old Bean Hill Road" is printed herein by permission of L. Leaf.

Michelle Lerner: "Sheltering Henry" is printed herein by permission of Michelle Lerner.

Lyn Lifshin: "Rowdy and Bleating" first appeared in *Yellow Bat*, #4, Fall 2002, and is reprinted herein by permission of Lyn Lifshin.

Ellaraine Lockie: "An Act of Kindness" appeared in *GOODRICHIE, Waterways, Contrarywise: An Anthology, Quill and Parchment, Chiron Review*, and *Poetry Super Highway*, was featured on *Your Daily Poet*, and is reprinted herein by permission of Ellaraine Lockie. "Bipolar" appeared in *Ibbetson Street* and in her chapbook, *Stroking David's Leg* (FootHills Publishing, 2009), and it is reprinted herein by permission of Ellaraine Lockie. "Sitcom in a Café" appeared in *EDGZ* and in *Main Channel Voices*, and it is reprinted herein by permission of Ellaraine Lockie.

Ronald Pies: "Missing Man" is printed herein by permission of Ronald Pies.

Kevin Pilkington: "Apple Spider" first appeared in *Inkwell*, Issue 11, Winter 2000, and is reprinted herein by permission of Kevin Pilkington. "Parthenon" first appeared in *Valparaiso Review*, Volume VII, Number 1, Fall/Winter 2006, and is reprinted herein by permission of Kevin Pilkington.

Lucas Pingel: "Coloring Death" and "Maria Dances and All I Can Do Is Drink" are printed herein by permission of Lucas Pingel.

Patricia Polak: "Bombazine" and "Caravan-ing" and "Urban Homesteading" are printed herein by permission of Patricia Polak.

Connie Post: "By the Window" first appeared in *The Carquinez Poetry Review*, Issue 4, 2006, and is reprinted herein by permission of Connie Post.

Julie Preis: "I catch the droplet in midair on its way to my lap." is printed herein by permission of Julie Preis.

Doug Ramspeck: "Jukebox Dancing" first appeared in *Clark Street Review*, 2006, and is reprinted herein by permission of Doug Ramspeck. "River Woman" first appeared in *Off the Coast*, 2006, and is reprinted herein by permission of Doug Ramspeck. "The Possessed" first appeared in *Epicenter*, 2008, and is reprinted herein by permission of Doug Ramspeck. "Strip Mall Apocalypse" is printed herein by permission of Doug Ramspeck.

Charles P. Ries: "Birch Street" first appeared in *Nerve Cowboy* in 2001, and is reprinted herein by permission of Charles P. Ries. "Los Huesos" first appeared in *Anthology 2000*, where it received a nomination for a Pushcart Prize, and is reprinted herein by permission of Charles P. Ries.

Amy Henry Robinson: "First Kiss" is printed herein by permission of Amy Henry Robinson.

E. M. Schorb: "The Man Who Hated Cities" first appeared in the *Palo Alto Review*, Fall 2005, and is reprinted herein by permission of E. M. Schorb. "The Souls" first appeared in *Stand*, Autumn 1997 (UK), and is reprinted herein by permission of E. M. Schorb.

Troy Schoultz: "Big Cats and Saxophone" is printed herein by permission of Troy Schoultz.

Anthony Seidman: "Cosmic Weather" first appeared in the online journal, *The Jivin' Ladybug*, and is reprinted herein by permission of Anthony Seidman.

Madeline Sharples: "Dream World" first appeared in the online journal, *Mamazine*, 2006, and is reprinted herein by permission of Madeline Sharples.

Eileen Sheehan: "I Asked My Love" first appeared in *The Cork Literary Review*, Vol. 9, later appeared in her poetry collection, *Song of the Midnight Fox* (Doghouse Books, 2004), and is reprinted herein from *Song of the Midnight Fox* by permission of Doghouse Books.

Michael Shorb: "Water Planet" is printed herein by permission of Michael Shorb.

Raymond Southall: "Round Dance" is printed herein by permission of Raymond Southall.

Dee Sunshine: "Frankfurt Airport" first appeared in his poetry collection, *Dropping Ecstasy with the Angels* (Bluechrome Publishing, 2004, UK) under his former nom-de-plume, Dee Rimbaud, and is reprinted herein by permission of Dee Sunshine.

Lois Swann: "Taking Possession" and "Thanksgiving" are printed herein by permission of Lois Swann.

Julie M. Tate: "Voyeur" is printed herein by permission of Julie M. Tate.

Sam Taylor: "The Lost World" first appeared in *New Orleans Review*, Volume 24, Number 3, 1998, later appeared in his poetry collection, *Body of the World* (Ausable Press, 2005), and is reprinted herein by permission of Sam Taylor. "The Undressing Room" first appeared in *Poetry Internationl*, Issue 10, 2006, later appeared in *Body of the World*, and is reprinted herein by permission of Sam Taylor.

Arlene Tribbia: "Aunt Julia's Lover" is printed herein by permission of Arlene Tribbia.

Vernon Waring: "The Rescue of Natalie Wood" first appeared in the online journal, *Ascent Aspirations Magazine*, Volume 12, Issue 4, November 2008, and is reprinted herein by permission of Vernon Waring.

Sarah Brown Weitzman: "The History of Red" and "The Painter" are printed herein by permission of Sarah Brown Weitzman.

Philip Wexler: "Night of Down" first appeared in *Other Voices*, Volume 14, #2, Winter 2001, and is reprinted herein by permission of Philip Wexler. "Flying White" and "Hard Drive" and "Potato Salad" and "Their Morning in Flannels" are printed herein by permission of Philip Wexler.

Les Wicks: "Under the Weather" first appeared in *Stories of the Feet* (Five Islands, 2004), and is reprinted herein by permission of Les Wicks.

Daniel Williams: "Citrus" is printed herein by permission of Daniel Williams.

A. D. Winans: "The Old Italians of Aquatic Park" first appeared in his book of poems, *The Other Side of Broadway* (Presa :S: Press, 2007), and is reprinted herein by permission of A. D. Winans.

Chris Wright: "The Blessed" is printed herein by permission of Chris Wright.

Martin Zehr: "On the Loose" is printed herein by permission of Martin Zehr.

Larry Ziman: "Bar Serendip" is printed herein by permission of Larry Ziman.

Fredrick Zydek: "Father Dancing" first appeared in *Sojourners*, March/April 1996, later appeared in 1998 in *Rural Voices: Anthology of Nebraska Poems*, also appeared in his poetry collection, *T'Kopachuck: The Buckley Poems* (The Winthrop Press, 2009), and is reprinted herein from *T'Kopachuck: The Buckley Poems* by permission of The Winthrop Press. "The Death of Plecostomus" first appeared in *Poetry Northwest*, 1974, later appeared in his poetry collection, *Lights Along the Missouri* (University of Nebraska Press, 1977), and is reprinted herein by permission of Fredrick Zydek. "The Boy Who Lived on Perkins Street" and "The House on A Street" and "The Line Dance of Field Ants" are printed herein by permission of Fredrick Zydek.

# Notes

# Notes

# Notes

# Notes

# Notes

# Notes